MW01603050

The Solution is at Hand
THE DOTTIE WALTERS STORY

Praise for "The Solution is at Hand: The Dottie Walters Story"

Dottie was truly an icon in the speaking world--one of a kind! Thanks for sharing her secrets with us in this superb literary work.
-- Irwin Zucker, Founder/Pres. Emeritus, Book Publicists of So. Calif. Pres., Promotion in Motion

Sharing Ideas is the name of Dottie Walters' magazine. It is also the creed Dottie's lived by. This book is her way of helping you find your solutions. Throughout history, we've had many heroes. A hero to us all is Dottie Walters - teaching so many of us how to find our solutions. Terri Marie has captured those teachings, providing a place where each of us can read and follow them.

Many times great people leave us and take their wisdom with them. This book is a great collection of the magic of Dottie Walters and her special way of teaching us how to solve problems. With this book, her magic is our magic.

A hearty "Thank You" to Terri Marie for immortalizing the teachings of Dottie Walters. Dottie helped people all her life. Now she can continue to do so.
--Jack Nichols
ML Innovative Properties, Inc. President

Dorothy, how does it feel to be a girl who has just blown to the world a blast of inspirational stardust?
--Napoleon Hill

Meeting Dottie Walters and Terri Marie was not only a fantastic experience but a great inspiration as well. I can now prolong and benefit from that experience by reading and rereading The Solution is at Hand: The Dottie Walters Story. A "MUST" read.
--John Harricharan
Author, When You Can Walk on Water, Take the Boat

Dottie was a catalyst for a lot of people. She made it possible for my bureau to grow and prosper. Now we can read her legacy in her amazing life story The Solution is at Hand: The Dottie Walters Story.
--Joseph I. Kessler, President, World Class Speakers & Entertainers

Dottie Walters has that special talent of putting thoughts into words that go out and move people. In addition to being a world-class expert at what she does, Dottie is a kind, loving person who has never for a moment lost her human touch.
--Earl Nightingale

The Solution is at Hand
THE DOTTIE WALTERS STORY

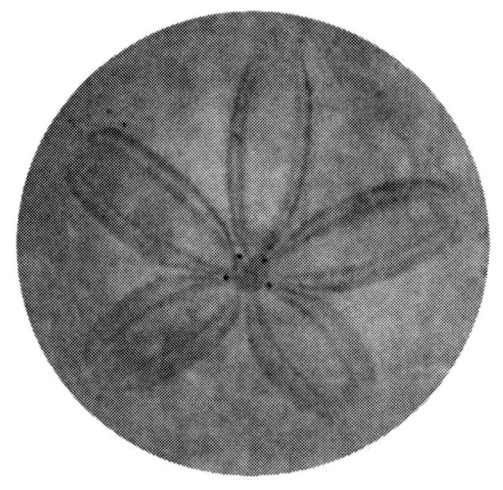

How to Look For and Find Opportunities

Dottie Walters & Terri Marie

The Solution is at Hand, The Dottie Walters Story, by Dottie Walters and Terri Marie

Library and Archives Cataloguing in Publication;

Walters Dottie and Marie, Terri
     The Solution is at Hand, The Dottie Walters Story / by Dottie Walters and Terri Marie.

ISBN 978-0-943477-14-5

1. Biography. 2. Self - Personal Growth – Success 3. Self – Motivation & Inspiration I. Title.

For additional information about quantity discounts, autographed books, and special promotions, please contact New World Publishing at www.insight2000.com, Walters Speakers Bureau at www.speakandgrowrich.com or White Wing Entertainment at www.spiritualarena.com

Dedicated to Jack Nichols
for introducing me to this once-in-a-lifetime lady.

For librarians everywhere who open the
gates to the wisdom of the world

WITH GRATITUDE

The authors wish to thank:

Jack Nichols for making the introduction.

The Walters Speakers Bureau:
Deborah Acero and **Michael MacFarlane**.

Jeanine Miranda for your help with this project.

John Harricharan of New World Publishing for your kindness.

All those who helped in the interviews sharing their stories and insights about Dottie.

Thank you for being part of the Dottie Walters Story.

CONTENTS

PART I
The Solution is at Hand:
The Dottie Walters Story

Dottie the Boss 31
The Look of Success 32
The Friendly Words 34
Hospitality Newsletter 34
Ask For What You Deserve..36

CHAPTER 7 Her First Book 37

The Nonexistent Book..38
Never Underestimate the Selling Power of THIS Woman 38
Her Second Big Break: The Meeting With Doctor Peale.........38
Cover Girl..39

CHAPTER 8 More Fame 42

The Seven Secrets of Selling To Women 42
Seven Roses 45
To Tell the Truth or Not 45

CHAPTER 9 The View From the Top of the Speaking World 49

Her Catapult to the Conventions 49
Speaking of Dottie..50
The Soft Sell..51
A Giving Voice 53
What it Means to Sell 53
What Do Women Want 54
Crumpled No More 55

CHAPTER 10 Bureaus and Sharing Ideas 59

The Queen of Speakers Bureaus..59
NSA Great Los Angeles Chapter 59
Founded in 1984 by Dottie Walters 59
Speaker Bureaus Unite 61
Sharing Ideas..64
Speaking Advice...64
Here are the Traits Dottie Feels a Speaker Should Have 66
Visualize Solutions...66
Her Brilliant Connection 67

PART II
Dottie's Life Lessons

PART I
The Solution is at Hand:
The Dottie Walters Story

Dottie Walters

Foreword
for Dottie Walters - *The Solution Is at Hand: The Dottie Walters Story*

by Jack Canfield
Co-creator of the *Chicken Soup for the Soul*® series   and Author of *The Success Principles*.

I first met Dottie Walters at a National Speakers Association meeting over 20 years ago. I was immediately struck by her deep wisdom, her generous spirit, and her amazing breadth of knowledge about speaking and writing. I was just breaking into the world of professional paid speaking after years as a high school teacher and trainer of teachers. I eagerly signed up for Dottie's magazine for speakers, *Sharing Ideas*, and would wait eagerly every month for its arrival so that I could learn more about how to take my message of self-esteem and self-empowerment to more and more people. I would read every article, underlining all of the ideas that I wanted to put into motion. I ordered the books that were reviewed and I read all the ads and ordered cassette tapes, manuals and anything else that I thought would help. I somehow knew I could trust Dottie and the people and resources she recommended and endorsed. I could just feel her sincere desire to help.

Years later, I moved to the Los Angeles area and actually got to visit Dottie in her home in Glendora. I was treated like an old friend visiting. My love and respect for Dottie grew deeper. Over the years, Dottie and I have crossed paths many times. Her wonderful story "Failure? No! Just Temporary Setbacks" appears in our first *Chicken Soup for the Soul* book, which was translated into 47 languages and has sold more than ten million copies around the world. Later, like a boyhood dream coming true, Dottie featured me on the cover of *Sharing Ideas* in 1992 and Mark Victor Hansen, my *Chicken Soup* co-author, and me again in 1995. Dottie and her daughter Lilly's book *Speak and Grow Rich* is like a bible among professional speakers, and I have told literally thousands of wannabe speakers to study that book if they want to be successful.

Dottie is more than a personal friend. She is an icon of success who shows you what possibilities in life might unfold for you, if you follow her example and *never give up*. Dottie's remarkable story and the stories of the people she has mentored would fill an entire *Chicken Soup for the Soul* book.

Through her books, speeches, articles and seminars, Dottie has empowered hundreds of thousands of people with an expanded awareness of their own potential for greatness. And now Dottie Walters and Terri Marie have joined forces to write a book that shows you the magnificent gem you have within when you use the power of your mind. They deliver many powerful strategies for success, including how Dottie uses the power of visualization, which I consider to be one of the most powerful tools that exist to facilitate and accelerate your success.

I know you are going to get great value from all fourteen wonderful Life Lessons from Dottie's story. My favorite is "Never Give Up!" because that has been probably the most profound lesson I received from Dottie over the years. When Mark and I went to New York to sell the first *Chicken Soup for the Soul* book to a publisher, we were rejected by all 22 publishers we met with. We were then rejected by 122 more over the course of the next 14 months. That's a lot of rejection. But, like Dottie, we believed in our dream and we believed in our message, so we rejected the rejections and kept saying "Next!" until we finally got a yes. Dottie's life exemplifies that spirit of persistence better than anyone I have ever met. I know you will be as inspired by her indomitable spirit as much as I have been.

My first mentor was a man named W. Clement Stone, a self-made multi-millionaire who also published *Success Magazine* back in the 1960s and '70s. He was truly an amazing man, and I was blessed that he shared so many of his secrets of success with me when I was so young. One of his key success principles was to learn from OPE—other people's experiences. He taught me to read biographies and autobiographies of famous people and to devour self help books of all kinds. He taught me that you can quantum leap your rise to success if you don't have to learn all of life's lessons from your own experience. You can borrow from the experience of others.

And now Dottie Walters, who has led an extraordinary life of service and accomplishment, has gifted you with this book so that you can learn from her experience how to find the opportunities that are always all around you, especially when a situation seems hopeless.

Dottie Walters is one of the great speakers and authors of our era, and as a woman who faced and triumphed over seemingly insurmountable odds as a young mother with two children in the middle of a financial crisis, her story is especially inspiring for all of us who have ever been faced with overwhelming challenges.

Dottie has always had kind of a Midas touch—putting the golden touch of success on every life she touches. And now she can do that for you in *The Solution Is at Hand: The Dottie Walters Story*. Dottie's greatest joy has always come from when she can give someone an idea that inspires them. So I know she must be very happy now, for here is a whole book full of ideas that will inspire you and encourage you to fully be all that you are, strive to become all you can be, and create the kind of fulfilling and meaningful life that you have dreamed of.

You are about to embark on a wonderful journey with a remarkable woman. Enjoy the ride, and when you are finished, I know you will love, admire, appreciate and respect Dottie Walters as much as I do.

Jack Canfield
Co-creator of the *Chicken Soup for the Soul*® series and author of *The Success Principles*.

Introduction

It has been my great privilege to meet Dottie Walters and an even greater privilege to call her my dear friend. There are few people on this earth with the insights and compassion of this grand woman. The gift she is about to share with you in this book is full of treasures that will help you think better, live richer and discover opportunities everywhere.

Dottie got her lessons and challenges early in life from both her negative and positive experiences with people. She turned them all into gold by never giving up and by always holding fast to her goals. Few people have lived as amazing a life. From her beginnings in the "little chicken ranching town" of Baldwin Park, California, to becoming perhaps the most respected woman speaker of her era, Dottie graced the stages of our time with elegance, humor, and class. But most importantly, she always gave audiences...love.

As you look at Dottie's life, you will see examples of how she was *always* able to look for and find answers. She loves to tell stories about the people who have influenced her. Dottie gives you many specific ideas and strategies for success. You hear the music of success dancing around her. Through her stories, insights, and the deep love she constantly gives, some of that success she has gathered, gets transferred to you. Then success can start to work through you, in the special way that only YOU can contribute to life.

When I did this series of interviews with Dottie for this book, one thing I always noticed was how magnificent her voice is. It is filled with energy and love. It's filled with the many experiences of success that she's had. That voice of hers has helped many people on their way to success.

When you get to the soda fountain story, notice Dottie's thinking process when she was faced with obstacle after obstacle. Then notice how she found and saw an opportunity when a chapter for her book was deleted. Dottie got her ideas everywhere. So can you. She will show you how.

When Dottie becomes your friend, she is your biggest cheerleader, strategist, and mentor. This book was very important to Dottie to have completed. Originally we were only going to do a CD set, but Dottie "insisted" in her friendly way, that I write a book. Once I agreed, she relaxed about it. She wanted to reach out to you through this book, to help you and encourage you in a different realm than her other books on specific subjects like selling or promoting (which she brilliantly wrote by the way.) This book is about life and living it as grand and glorious as possible. Dottie wanted to share what she has been blessed to learn. You can create a life as magnificent as Dottie's. That's why we wrote this book.

When I asked Dottie what we should call our project together, she didn't hesitate, "The Solution is at Hand," Dottie said. It's about being open to possible answers for the unknown challenges you will face. If you can look at each "problem" in your life and see that the solution is already there, you will be able to rise to the top in whatever field you wish. You will have an air of expectancy and excitement around problems after reading Dottie's story because you'll be able to think another way about them. You ABSOLUTELY will know there is an answer, a perfect "solution" that is waiting for you to find it. You may have to work for it, reach for it or think for it...but it *is* there. The challenge is your gift. When you get a challenge, you can be assured you are being asked to grow.

Sometimes what we need more than anything in life is hope. The greatest leaders have always offered that to people. In "The Solution is at Hand," Dottie will tell you answers to questions like "How do you pay attention to the good voices in your mind?" and "How do you notice opportunities?" The answers may surprise you.

Our world of today needs big solutions and big answers. Answers we haven't thought of yet. It is by all of us learning to think in a new way about these new answers that we'll be able to rise to reach them, to "think" towards the solution God is urging us to find. Dottie has always asked for help from her friends of the mind. What would Ben Franklin do? What would Einstein do? Now what will you do? - for *your* solution is in your hands.

This is my meager attempt to capture the grand lady's life.

Terri Marie
Author of "Be the Hero of Your Own Game."

CHAPTER 1
It Was There From the Start

Dottie and her Mother Lil

She was a New Year's Eve baby. Born at the very end of one cycle and the start of another, Dottie appeared at the cusp of an era of great opportunity. It seemed to be the theme of her life.

It was only a few years ago that I met Dottie Walters. It doesn't take long for this lady to have a huge impact on your life. My friend, Jack Nichols, had been telling me about this special lady he knew. One day he made arrangements to take me up to see her at her home, "the ranch" as it is known to all who have been there. I didn't know what to expect from Dottie, but I instantly liked her. After some initial consulting, we became good friends. We often went to meetings together where we had many wonderful hours to discuss life. I'd go back with her and spend the night in her lovely guest room at the ranch. She was always concerned about me driving back to San Clemente late at night. In the morning in her cozy family room, we'd chat. I'd hear story after story, lesson after lesson.

Terri Marie and Dottie at "The Ranch."

Dottie loved flowers. We'd walk around her Spanish style home looking at her roses and colorful flowers. She'd show me her garden and the special area where she has her little Scottish castle. Once a bunch of crows were up on the power lines squawking as we were talking. Out of the blue. Dottie looked at me and said, "You suppose they're sending us messages?"

Dottie was born in Los Angeles and has always lived in Southern California. Today she lives in Glendora. Dottie had no brothers or sisters. She once told me that's why her friends in the speaking world mean so much to her. Speaking gave her the opportunity to make friends across the globe and turn her audiences everywhere into people she loved and that loved her. Dottie so easily makes you feel like family.

Dottie always had a flair for business and for life. Like a master who lived many years ago, she loves to tell stories. One of the many stories that Dottie told me that I love (and it tells a lot about her) is when she was a mere three years old. She was at the beach with her mother when her mother couldn't find little Dottie.

The Littlest Entrepreneur

Her mother, Lil, had bought Dottie a bright red bathing cap. "It looked like a bucket. It hung over my eyebrows," laughed Dottie. Her mother had also bought Dottie a little pail and shovel for their upcoming beach trip. Lil and her two friends were going down to Laguna Beach in California. Her mother told Dottie that the ladies were going to put up an umbrella and set out a blanket to sit on. But first she told Dottie to come down to the edge of the water because she wanted to show Dottie something. That sure piqued Dottie's curiosity. The little three-year-old gal went willingly down to the shore.

Dottie's mother took the little shovel and started digging in the sand. Magical, white, round shells appeared. Her mother told her they were "sand dollars." The sand dollars fascinated Dottie. She saw what looked like a little flower in the center of them. "They were pure white and so pretty," Dottie remembers. She asked her mother if she could put some in her bucket. Her mother said okay, but told Dottie to stay right there and dig for them, while she went back up to give her friends a hand with the umbrella. It looked like they were having a lot of trouble with it. She told Dottie she would be back in just a few minutes.

When her mother got up to where the ladies were struggling with the umbrella, one of her mother's friends said, "Lil, She's gone!" referring to Dottie. Dottie's mother screamed and ran back to the shore. She thought Dottie had gotten pulled out to sea. She yelled for the lifeguards. The lifeguards came running down and swam out to look for the little child in the red bathing cap. The big waves were rolling into the California shore, but no Dottie. Then one of her mother's friends said, "Lil, turn around and look the other way. There is someone with a red bathing cap on up there." It was little Dottie, up on the wooden boardwalk in Laguna Beach. Her mother came running up, screaming at her, more out of fear than anger, "Dorothy Mae, what are you doing?" Dottie had piles of pennies with all the shells laid out and proudly stated; "I'm giving these people sand dollars for just pennies!"

Even at three years old she had an enterprising spirit. Dottie knew what value was and wasn't afraid to offer it to people. "You can give a product that's worth dollars for pennies even now," says Dottie, "but you have got to go and get things that are worth more. Then people will be glad to pay you. Don't keep saying 'I'm no good.' Quit that!"

Fairy Tales

Dottie has another fond memory of Laguna Beach where her family once owned a cabin in the canyon. In the summertime, Laguna Beach held an outdoor theater. They were putting on a play and Dottie was chosen as a very small child to perform as a little "fairy." The girls dressed in white, wispy gowns and hid among the tall trees giggling until their cue to come out. They watched a very large Friar Tuck sing as he stirred a big pot. Their job as fairies was to run out and push Friar Tuck over, which they did to great laughter. This gave Dottie practice for her future mission. This little pixie would eventually grow up to push over one of the most solid societal structures ever set in place – and give women a place in the world of selling and speaking. Those lessons from her childhood would prove enormously valuable to Dottie's coming success.

CHAPTER 2
The Early Influencers

Books Were Her Doorway
to Success

One of Dottie's many Ben Franklin images.

Dottie grew up loving to read. She subscribed to *"Wee Wisdom"* magazine as a child and read every issue from cover to cover. Later she loved to read biographies. The librarians at her local library got to know the young Dottie because her mother took Dottie there at least once a week. She was a voracious reader, hungry for knowledge and inspiration. Dottie started reading book series like the *Lad* stories about the dog. After she finished one series of books, the librarian would say, "I have another series for you. Then Dottie would move onto the next series. She read them all.

When Dottie told the librarian that she was going into high school, the librarian took Dottie up to a room in the library that she'd never been to before - the room of biographies. The librarian told Dottie, "I have an assignment for you. This is the room where we have all the books on people of achievement." Dottie was thrilled as she climbed up that stairway. Now she'd be able to read about the adventures of incredible people throughout time. After the librarian unlocked the room, Dottie stared at walls filled to the ceiling with books. That special librarian told her, "All the people who have achieved great things are waiting to talk to you in this room. I want you to start over here and read every book in the room!" And of course, Dottie did read every single book in that room!

An Author Reaches Beyond Time

Dottie loves to tell what happened to her when she first entered that room of biographies. "I put my hand down," she said, "and the very first one I reached for was Benjamin Franklin's autobiography - right at hand - which is where opportunity always is! It was kind of sticking out a little bit. I think he was waiting for me! He's one of my great *Friends of the Mind*. I read his book and of course, fell in love with him." Ben was the first, but not the only author to influence Dottie in that kind of way.

A Friend of the Mind

Those authors in that room would deeply influence her life with their wisdom. Dottie gained tremendous knowledge about life from Ben Franklin's book. She said, "I learned that you never give up, you think of another way to do things, and there's always another solution at hand." Dottie deeply admired Ben's abilities, especially as a great inventor. She was astonished that he figured out a new way to measure the river that's in the ocean. When they finally laid the first telephone lines from Europe to Nova Scotia, they used Franklin's charts. It was at least a hundred years later when they laid those transatlantic lines. Dottie knew that Ben was way ahead of his time. She admired forward thinking people and Franklin certainly was one of them. She loved Ben's inner vision. He was constantly looking ahead to think of other ways to do things. Soon, Dottie started to think like Ben. He taught her his wisdom through his books.

Dottie has the wonderful ability to take history and make it into a story. She can bring it alive with the essence of the tale as if it were happening in our time, not in a bland, lifeless past. Dottie laughs about Ben's ingenuity and how he'd find a way around things. She said Ben loved to write. Ben's brother put out a newspaper but told Ben he couldn't write for it, because the brother didn't think Ben had the ability. Not to be discouraged, Ben wrote under a "Nom de Plume." He called himself, "Silence Dogood." He wrote as a humorous, middle-aged widow with a sarcastic bent. Ben could cleverly state opinions with his pseudonym that would never be accepted coming from the young Ben who was a mere sixteen years old at the time. At night, after he'd written an article, Ben would slip out and put the article under the front door of the newspaper. His brother didn't find out for a long time - after he had printed many of "Ben's" articles. The articles were a big hit but when his brother found out, he got mad. He would've silenced poor "Silence Dogood but unfortunately Ben's brother was sent to jail for his views against the government. Ben was able to pen 15 articles before he himself silenced the outspoken "Silence." Dottie told me many more stories about Ben, all illustrating his resourcefulness, playfulness and ingenuity. He was always thinking of how life can be improved. Dottie liked that. She was especially pleased that he started a library in Philadelphia that's still in use today. Ben had success writing as a woman. Dottie broke into the man's world of selling by writing *about* women. Even though she went into a man's world, Dottie always maintained her femininity.

The Scene on the Porch

Just as Dottie was ready to go into high school, her father left home. Her parents were out on the front porch screaming at each other. Dottie's mother asked, "What about this girl going to college?" referring to Dottie. Dottie's father yelled, "She is too stupid to ever be accepted into any college!" "They were saying it so loud that I knew all of the neighbors could hear what he said," Dottie said. "With that, he left us." After all this time, with all of her brilliant achievements, it's still a tender spot with Dottie.

Dottie never mentioned her father except for the story on the porch included here. When I asked Dottie's daughter, Jeanine her grandfather's name, she couldn't even remember it. Jeanine said. "He was awful." Enough said.

Throughout her high school years, Dottie's father never paid a penny of support to the family, not even food money. "I just felt so down about that," Dottie said. "But when I went in and talked to Benjamin Franklin, he didn't tell me that. He didn't tell me that at all! He said, 'If you can plan it and work at it, you can do it.' You see, he's always thinking of what's possible, not impossible." That had a huge influence on Dottie. She learned to pay attention to Franklin's encouraging voice, not her father's. "We can all do that," Dottie says speaking of which voice we choose to pay attention to. "We all have access to any mind there is. And my father was wrong," said Dottie resolutely.

Even though he was wrong, her father left some scars, not just emotional. He used to hit Dottie with a ruler while trying to make her learn math. "To this day I have an adding machine on my desk," she says. "It still bothers me a great deal, because he was so cruel. That doesn't help anybody to learn anything." Dottie certainly was not stupid. She let go of the cruel man and focused on the kind, inspiring one. Today she honors the gentle and wise Ben with a wall of Ben Franklin in her home on the stairs by her office. She'd often point out Ben's photo to me and remark how his mouth was turned up at the sides, just like he was ready to burst into a smile.

CHAPTER 3
Solutions

It Began at The "Moor"

Another display of her ingenuity was when she was working nights at a bakery while she was in high school. That entrepreneurial spark of hers was just waiting to become fully ignited, but it was already showing it's potential.

One of Dottie's English teachers had the class write a continuation of the story about one of the characters in Dickens, "A Tale of Two Cities." The teacher liked Dottie's story so much that she read it to the class. "I was so thrilled to think that she would choose mine to read!" said Dottie. When her teacher got through reading it, she said, "This girl will be advertising manager and feature editor for the Alhambra High School paper *The Moor*, starting next semester." "Oh gosh, I felt like I was sailing around the room," said Dottie. "I was so excited and proud."

The teacher told Dottie after class, that she needed to have her first articles ready to turn in along with a plan of how she was going to lay the pages out, by the next morning. But Dottie had a job right after school. She had worked since her father left the family without any support. Dottie explained to the teacher that she needed her job. She had to help her mother because the family didn't have much income. But this was not an opportunity Dottie was about to pass up either.

A Sticky Situation

That evening Dottie got on the school bus. It let her off at the Midnight Market where she worked in the bakery. Dottie's job was not glamorous. She had to clean all the big glass cases, scrub the floors, fold boxes for the next day, and then dump the garbage out back in the dumpster. While at work, she got as far as the dumpster, and started thinking about her homework assignment. "Where am I going to find some paper? I don't know where to get it," she thought. "I kept looking and thinking, 'Who's got paper?' I thought maybe the guys in the meat department might have some. I was going to ask them, but when I got out back to the trash bin, I noticed lots of bags that had been thrown away because they had gotten sticky." If the worker got a little frosting on his or her thumb trying to put things in the bag, then the bag got sticky so they couldn't give it to the customers. They had to give them a new one. Dottie saw that there was quite a stack of clean sheets of "paper" if the sticky part was torn off. She gathered the bags and started writing her assignment that was due the next morning on those bakery bags. Her teacher said, "Wow! I've never had a student that brought their homework in on a bakery bag before!" "The solution was at hand!" Dottie said. "At hand. It was right there! Like most things it was right there in front of you."

About that story that Dottie wrote on those bakery bags. She wrote about the pharmacist in "The Tale of Two Cities." The real murderer in the story had been set free. Dottie wrote that he had come to the pharmacist to make a decision regarding the fate of the man who resembled him. It foreshadowed one of the most tremendous opportunities of her life.

CHAPTER 4
Her Big Break - Sole Power

Dottie and Bob Walters on their wedding day

The Marine She Loved

Dottie recently spoke at a Book Publicists of Southern California meeting. They loved her great knowledge and willingness to help other authors succeed. One of the men attending that meeting had been a Marine in WWII. He showed her a book that described the battle in Tarawa, Japan that her husband, Bob fought in. Dottie really wanted to get a copy of that book. But when she did and read the story as written in the book, she told me, "That's not how Bob told me it happened." Here's how it happened.

Bob Walters, Dottie's soon-to-be husband, had just gotten back from four years in the South Pacific in the Marine Corps. She said, "He was a staff sergeant in the Second Marine Division and in all the major battles. The last battle he was in was Tarawa, Japan."

Tarawa was described as "one of the most vicious battles in American history," by Navy Journalist, William Polson. "In three days over 1000 Americans lay dead on a flat sandy area smaller than New York's Central Park." Bob and his captain had gotten off the boats but they didn't realize how shallow the bay was at Tarawa. The boats were hitting the bottom. The men had to hold their ammunition and guns over their heads as they walked to the shore. The Japanese had machine guns and were strafing the water.

"The captain and my fiancée got about half way in," Dottie tells, "and they looked back. They saw their own men going down. So they immediately turned around and went back for them. Together they brought in man after man." There was a medical unit set up on the island where Bob and the captain took the wounded men. For that act, Bob received a Presidential Citation. Bob told Dottie how hard it was. Some of the guys who were hit pretty badly had told him, "Don't let my wallet get wet because it has my sweetheart's picture in it." It was because of Bob's courage and his willingness to take action when it really mattered (two traits Dottie has always admired) that they were able to save a lot of men because they were able to get them in fast enough to the medical unit on the island. That was a real hero. Dottie never forgot his bravery,

Bob had been on the ground, right in the reefs. The story he told Dottie was from that perspective. The one in the book was from a pilot. So they each saw a different scene. Dottie was so hopeful that there would be a picture of her beloved Bob in that book. That may have been the most disappointing to her of all.

Bob and Dottie's daughter, Jeanine said of her father, "Like most WWII vets, he didn't talk much about it because he wanted to protect everyone. We were watching a special on TV once. The Japanese were making a resort out of Tarawa and they had moved the WWII monument. It was one of the few times I saw my father cry."

Dottie and Bob had written to each other every day the whole time he was gone. After those four years, they were married when he returned to California. The young couple settled in the small town of Baldwin Park.

The Opportunity in Disguise

Bob Walters bought a dry cleaning franchise when he came back from the war. He'd been in that field before he went into the service and he knew a lot about the business. Bob tried to open up new routes, but found out that there had been a big decline in the economy in Southern California. Nobody was having any dry cleaning done. They would just sponge things off and hang them outside to air out. Then they'd wear them again.

Dottie describes a particular day when fate interceded in her life. "Bob came home one evening and he just looked so beat," she said. "He sat down on the couch and put his head down on his hands. In a moment I saw... that he was crying. He was sobbing! Here this brave, brave man was crying. I went and put my arms around him and said, 'Honey what is it? What's wrong?' He said, 'I can't make the house payment.' He said that he was trying so hard and had walked miles and miles trying to establish a dry cleaning route. Bob said, 'Nobody is buying any dry cleaning.'

Dottie prayed for a way to help her husband. She opened her bible to a quote. As often happened, a good book gave her the answer. This was the passage she read. "For unto everyone that hath, shall be given and he shall have abundance." She looked at what skills she had and thought about her shoppers column. Dottie told Bob, "You know, when I was in high school I worked on the high school newspaper in advertising, and I bet I could write a similar column here." They had a weekly paper, the *Baldwin Park Bulletin*, in the town. "'Would you mind if I did that?" she said. "I think I could help. Let's pull on the rope together." Bob, not knowing what else to do, just put his hands up in the air. It was Dottie's opportunity to show what she was made of.

Dottie's mind went to work. She sat down and made a list of what she needed. "It was a long list," she said. "I needed a typewriter, I didn't have any paper. I didn't have any shoes that weren't worn out. I thought, 'Boy, I've got to do something about those shoes first. So I went up to the grocery store that was just a couple of blocks away, and asked the owner if I could please have some cardboard boxes. He gave me several of them. I drew a little outline of my shoe and put the cardboard in my shoes. I took a bunch of extra cardboard liners with me because I thought they might wear out. You see, in Baldwin Park, they only had a paved street where the stores were. But where the track homes were, the streets were all made of gravel. The gravel would chop up the shoes."

As she got everything ready to go, a signal that she was on the right track appeared. A free sample copy of the *Baldwin Park Bulletin* landed on her driveway. Dottie said, "Then I asked a neighbor if I could borrow her typewriter. She not only lent me her typewriter but gave me a whole stack of paper too! Those (500 sheets) were surely magic sheets of paper. I felt in that moment that I was flying on them around the world. I got my column and my samples from the high school ads that I had sold. I thought they'd surely offer me a job. I started to put the children in the stroller, and then I realized, my gosh they wouldn't fit! They'd grown too big for that stroller." But Dottie thought of Einstein's quote, "The solutions are at hand" and quickly improvised a seat. She grabbed a pillow from the bed, tied it to the stroller with some clothesline for a rope, plopped the other youngster in the newly made seat, and off they went to downtown Baldwin Park.

The Lesson in Use

"Every successful business started with a great obstacle."
Dottie Walters

Dottie's Grandpa Robert

Dottie had her big test early on. A lesson from her grandfather proved invaluable. "My Scottish Grandpa used to tell me when I was a little girl, 'Lassie, just remember. We Scotts never give up. We never give up!' I taught the children to say that, because as we got out on that gravel, the wheel came off the stroller. I said, 'What do we say children?' They would laugh like it was a game and say, 'We'll never give up! Take off your shoe, Mom!' I'd take off my shoe and use the heel - that's what shoes are for - and jammed that wheel back on again and off we went. That darn wheel came off quite often getting down there. I finally got to the newspaper office. There on the door was a great big sign saying 'No Help Wanted.' I stood there and said, 'Oh, no. They don't want me.' I was trying not to cry because I didn't want the children to see and think that I was going to give up. Suddenly my friend of the mind Benjamin Franklin came to me and spoke to me right there. He was a newspaperman, you know. He started the *Saturday Evening Post*. Ben said, 'Now Dottie, what's the matter? These people want you. Don't feel that you are being rejected. They just don't have the money to pay you. Don't ask for a job, ask for an opportunity!' Of course! I didn't think of that."

Armed with Ben's advice, Dottie went into the newspaper office pushing her children in the stroller. "They were very good sitting, watching and listening. I laid out everything I had prepared for the publisher and said, 'Here's what I would like to do. I would like to buy space from you at a wholesale rate. I'll go out and sell it. But the rate that I sell it to the merchants will be at the same rate that they could buy any ad from you, so I won't be undermining you with your customers. I will sell it and you will have an interesting column, different from anything you've ever had before. What do you think?' He said, 'Go for it girl.' So I did."

Dottie said of that opportunity, "I didn't know till the second I looked at him that I was going to say that. Pushing the children home that day I didn't know it, but I'd just made the most important sale of my life."

There at that newspaper was opportunity knocking it's little had off! Dottie heard it's familiar sound. She went to every store in town. Many of the storeowners liked the column. With that single act, Dottie had the beginnings of what would become a great business.

Wishes Can Come True

"When my mother and I were very poor, we'd go window shopping and we used to tell one another, 'We're window wishing.' My maiden name was Wells so I called my column, *Window Wishing with Wells*. It was quite a success." The column seemed to be her one talent. Dottie said, "I couldn't afford to hide it."

"I was shy and frightened but I tried to smile and think about my merchant's problems. I did restrict their ads to one each time on their first order to be sure they weren't buying out of sympathy for me. I tried to give each one something extra, a little special courtesy of some kind." Before long, Dottie was buying a double column. Her one talent was multiplying. Dottie never thought she was good at math, but she could multiply success better than anyone I know!

CHAPTER 5
The Fountain of Opportunity

There is a room in Dottie's ranch that is very special to her because of what's in it and how it got there.
It is her most famous story.

The Ahlman's Rexall Drug Store in Baldwin Park, CA

The Turning Point

One day Dottie went to solicit ads for her shopper's column from four merchants in Baldwin Park. She had previously tried to sell an ad to the local pharmacist in town who owned a Rexall Drug store. "Every time I'd go in, he was out. He was always out. I never could see him," she said. Those four different businesses told her, "You don't have the man that we most admire in town in your column. He is a fine man and if he's not using your column, then we don't want it either. Dottie thought, "Oh my gosh, I must try again! He must be working sometime. If he could just look at it and give me a comment, then I could give it to these merchants that know him and think so much of him."

The Walters tenacity kicked in. Her Scottish blood, inherited from that undaunted grandfather of hers, was moving her towards success. Dottie went back one more time to see if she could talk to that pharmacist. This time as she walked in the front, she could see that the back of the pharmacy was lit up. "There I saw him - white hair with the white jacket that they wear. I had my kids with me again. I walked up and said 'Mr. Ahlman, I don't want to sell you anything, I just want you to give me your thoughts on this column. Would you just be so kind as to look at it? The other merchants in town want your opinion. Please, would you?' He shook his head from left to right. His mouth was an upside down U, saying no."

"I thought that I didn't know if I could make it home and push the kids all the way up there. I got as far as the soda fountain. There were three empty stools. I sat down on the one closest to me and pulled the kids up close to me so they wouldn't be in the way. I just sat there thinking, 'What am I going to do?' The soda jerk came over. I asked him, 'How much for your smallest Coke?' It was 10 cents. That was all I had, so I laid that out and gave the kids an extra straw so they got a little sip. They were thirsty too, breathing all that dust."

The Angel by the Fountain

"Soon two ladies came in and sat down on the stools next to me. The one sitting closest to me turned and said, 'What in the world is wrong with you, girl?' I said, 'We are going to lose our home. I've done everything I can think of to do. Everyone thinks so much of Mr. Ahlman and he won't even give me his opinion on my column. Four merchants turned me away today. Those four would have finished the house payment. I don't want to lose our little house.' The lady said, 'You wait right here.' First she snatched away the column that I had in my hand. She read every word of it. Then she yelled, 'Rueben, get out here!' It was her husband!"

Mr. Ahlman, the pharmacist, proved to be truly generous to every charity. So much so, that his wife said that she'd be taking over that part of the business. Dottie had been talking to the wrong person! "I didn't know enough to know to ask who was in charge of that part of the business," Dottie said.

Mrs. Ahlman told her husband, "You give this girl copy for this week. I'll go back and make a check out for two months of ads." Dottie was stunned. Next, Mrs. Ahlman asked Dottie for the names of the four merchants who turned her away. As soon as Dottie gave her their names, Mrs. Alhman left to place phones calls to each one of them. She returned to tell Dottie that the merchants were waiting to see her. Dottie didn't give up. She looked for the opportunity. This one changed her life.

The biggest opportunities seem to have a special knack of only showing themselves when things seem at their bleakest, when life seems dark and out of options. This is where opportunity becomes visible if you open to it. At that moment you can ask for the opportunity to present itself. It will be happy to do so. Great opportunities are just waiting for moments like that. Dottie's was no different.

Dottie said, "Einstein was right. Solutions are located at hand. They are very close to you. But you have to go after them. They are not going to sit there by themselves and do it. You've got to do it. Reach out and don't be afraid to go do it, because it's waiting for you."

We did these interviews seated right next to Dottie's largest symbol of success - that soda fountain. It literally was right at hand. Eventually, the Ahlman's decided to take the soda fountain out of their drug store. Dottie's husband, Bob, bought it from them and installed it in their den. It used to be twice as long but it wouldn't fit in their den so they cut it down to 12 stools. They are the original stools that Dottie got her first big break on.

Every day. Dottie can look at that fountain and see the symbol of the start of her career. While no Hollywood director discovered Dottie, it was at a drug store that SHE discovered success and her own ability to persist until success gave up its glorious and well-deserved rewards to her.

The Ahlmans and Dottie

Dottie still feels immense gratitude when she points to the exact stool where she was sitting and to the stools where the two ladies sat. "That's where it began," Dottie told me. "She (Mrs. Ahlman) was waiting for me there. I was so glad that she was there when I came in."

Like an angel, Mrs. Ahlman appeared when Dottie needed that big opportunity. Bob and Dottie became very good friends with Mr. and Mrs. Ahlman. Dottie feels that certain people come into our lives at special moments to help us and Mrs. Ahlman was one of them. Take note. There is a Mrs. Alhman out there for each one of us.

CHAPTER 6
A Modern Day Business Cinderella

Dottie on stage

Serving and Speaking

Then Dottie got the idea that perhaps she could reach more merchants if she could speak to the service clubs. Dottie asked her advertisers if they belonged to any of the service clubs in town. Many of the clubs had a luncheon once a week, like the Kiwanis, Lions, or Rotary Clubs. This was enormously gutsy on her part. At that time women couldn't join the service clubs. They couldn't even open a charge account without their husband's signature. Here she was speaking to male only service clubs and giving them advice!

She'd learned early on in life a lesson that would affect how she did business. When Dottie was ten years old, a doll was to be given as a prize for a certain number of newspaper subscriptions sold. Dottie wanted that doll and set out to knock on doors till she got it. At one home, a large woman came to the door and said, "Just a minute, little girl. You want me to spend my money so you can get a doll?' "That woman scared me to pieces!" Dottie said. "She yelled so loud I took off running." Dottie learned early that you have to give your buyer a bargain or you won't make the sale. Since that day, she always put her sponsors needs first.

Dottie decided to give herself a moniker - a couple of words you put after your name. You always use it every time you sign your name. She called herself, *Dottie Walters, your customer.* She wanted the merchants to know that women, as the homemakers, were the customers for that little business section. When she spoke, she told her audience, "I want you to know what we think about when we walk into your store. We hope that you are looking for us, anxious to help us. How do you suppose we'd feel if you said, 'Ah help yourself.' We'd feel pretty rejected. Or if you say, 'We're closing in 5 minutes. You'll have to come back tomorrow.' You don't know how far we may have come to get here. I think that if you'd be loving and caring to your customers, you'll find that your customers will increase and tell their friends." Pretty good advice coming from the young Dottie Walters.

The merchants liked Dottie's approach and spunk. Everywhere she spoke, Dottie gave them a little card to fill out. She explained that she had a prize for a drawing. The first prize was a pretty little vase that she'd had since she was a little girl. Dottie gift wrapped it and said, "One of you is going to take this home to your wife today, but you have to fill the card out to be in the drawing." Dottie knew this would make one lucky man a hero to his wife. The comment card said, 'Yes, I'd like to talk to you about your shopper's column. Please call me. Here is the best day and the best time to call me.' The merchants signed it and put their phone numbers down. Then Dottie could follow up by phone because they had seen her and knew who she was. She was building a wealth of relationships. Dottie's *Window Wishing* shopper's column did very well because of the value it gave both the readers and the merchants.

Hospitality Hostess

"If you give the people around you "heart,"
you are giving them a great gift,"
Dottie Walters

Dottie welcoming a new resident.

Shortly after her great success with her column, Dottie received another fantastic opportunity. Some of the advertisers for her column appeared at her door with a big break for her. They knew they were coming to the right person. Programs like "Welcome Wagon" were springing up all over. The merchants thought that because of Dottie's successful column, she was in a perfect situation to start such a service in Baldwin Park. They offered to finance her. Never one to turn down a good opportunity, Dottie agreed and grew the business called *Hospitality Hostess Service* to offices all over Southern California, from Riverside to San Diego. "It was quite a job," she said, "with monthly meetings for each area." The merchants would come to the meetings. They'd often invite Dottie and her employees to tour their stores. Dottie said that it really helped them to provide better service to their clients.

Dottie brought along large geographical maps when she talked to her merchant sponsors. She'd unfold the maps and point out areas so they could see which areas they wanted to cover. Dottie used the soft sell and learned from her great friend Ben to ask questions like "Have you thought of...?" or "What did you plan to do with...?" When she asked why the merchants choose her to sponsor into business, they told Dottie it was because she always kept her promises. Her word was gold. That's one of the traits she looks for in those she surrounds herself with today.

Dottie fixed up a welcome basket with pretty flowers, lollipops, maps of the town, coupons from the merchants, free gifts, and civic literature. In her baskets were "What did you think of the store?" cards for newcomers to fill out and return to the store. The merchants loved this. It gave them feedback. When a new person moved into town, there would be a friendly, smiling Dottie at the door with a pretty gift for the woman of the house. Dottie talked to each woman as if she were her friend, which didn't take Dottie long to do. "Here is the biggest supermarket in town," Dottie would say as she pulled out a map of the town. "Your boy can attend Boy Scout meetings here and for your girl, the Girl Scouts meet here. Baldwin Park has fine churches." "When you call on one of your sisters," Dottie said, "talk to her like one."'

Dottie sent out the perfect message from Saint Matthew on her Christmas Letter: "And they loved him and the wise men opened their treasures and presented unto the newcomer, gifts." St. Matthew could have been talking about one wise woman named Dottie Walters.

You don't get away with much in a little town like Baldwin Park. "One of the things that helped me at that time," said Dottie "was the merchants. Word got around town that I was walking with those babies." Soon, Dottie's husband Bob was able to buy her a black model A Ford so she could make more calls. Dottie kept learning about the merchants and what they needed. "I made a lot of friends. The merchants were watching me. They saw that I was working. I had eight branch offices all over Southern California."

With Dottie's service, when you moved into a neighborhood, there was always someone there to greet you. Even famous people move to new cities. In San Diego, Dottie welcomed people like Mrs. Robert Wilder, wife of the famous author. Their meeting was covered in the local papers. Dottie grew her business larger than the famous *Welcome Wagon*.

A simple basket, connected businesses with newcomers in town and grew Dottie's business from 60 employees and 1500 advertisers, to 130 employees and 4,000 advertisers. Then it skyrocketed to 200 employees who made 5000 calls a month for 5000 merchants contracts. They served 300 cities. Dottie was busy.

One day Dottie was perming her hair when the bags she had left by the stove caught fire. In a rush to put the fire out, she laid the bottle of neutralizer down. When she got back, her son had the empty bottle in his hand. He had drunk it. Dottie rushed him to the hospital. Returning an hour later wondering if her unfinished perm would cause her hair to fall out, her husband Bob walked in and said casually, "What's new?" It struck Dottie so funny that she and Bob fell into each other's arms laughing. Bob told her, "Honey, I don't think this marriage will ever die of boredom." And as an aside, her son was fine and is a brilliant professional today.

Dottie brought on her first partner. Virginia Thompson, Dottie's neighbor, agreed to make half the house calls. They were very excited to work together and even had identical dresses. "Just like airlines stewardesses," said Dottie, thrilled with her new business partner. One morning Dottie got a call from Virginia's husband. Virginia had died suddenly in the night. Dottie deeply grieved the loss of her friend and in doing so she went back to her basics, Franklin and the Bible. In both she found an uplifting spirit and message as if "Someone had opened a window to let in clean sweet air."

Dottie at her first Hospitality House – where it all started.

Because the welcome service was booming and she was still writing her column, Dottie had to make a choice. "By the end of the week after Virginia's death, I knew I'd have to decide between the hostess service and the shopper's column. I couldn't handle both myself." Dottie dropped the column and focused on the *Hospitality Hostess* business, which would still allow her to work with the merchants. Eventually she moved the business into a house that her and Bob renovated into a charming gingerbread-style cottage. They called it the "Hospitality House."

Bob sold the dry cleaning business and began helping print the *Hospitality Hostess* books and coupons. He called it "Double H" Printing.

Dottie the Boss

Dottie training some of her hostesses

Dottie employed only positive people. I guess you could call them "Double P" people. She called them "plus people." One woman Dottie interviewed was struggling during the interview. Dottie was ready to stand up but instead Dottie held up her purse and asked the woman if she were selling it what would she say. The woman stumbled again. Dottie was ready to dismiss her, when the woman smiled and said cheerfully, "Besides, you'll love owning it. Look how it matches your shoes!" Dottie gave her the job. She became one of her top saleswomen.

But Dottie did not hire the woman who said, "Listen lady, when you're as old as I am, you'll take any lousy job that comes along."

An accountant Dottie had hired also had a very negative attitude. Dottie started to dread his visits. He'd tell her, "Why don't you give up Dottie? The job can't be done." Her answer? "The job can *always* be done some way. (Of course by saying that, *he* was the one who was quitting!) She let him go. "From then on I've tried to have only plus people around me," she said.

Dottie made the business fun for her staff. She had "Lulu" trees, which held earrings. Whenever a hostess had a birthday that month, she could choose a set of earrings from the tree.

The Look of Success

Dottie always looked great. Eventually, Dottie started to wear her famous hats. "I developed my trademark after I learned it helped me make a sale." There was a client Dottie wanted to sign up – a haberdasher - but she couldn't even get an interview. Dottie dressed up in a nice hat and paid him a visit. That got his attention. He became a client and told her, "The minute you walked in, I noticed you. I knew you were a lady because you were wearing a hat." If there is anything Dottie is, it's a lady. Those hats and her sincere interest in people became her trademark.

Dottie in one of her trademark hats

"When it rained I even had a red plastic raincoat for my basket and one for myself to match." Dottie dressed like a very successful woman, yet she remained feminine. Dottie dressed her children well too. "Growing up, I always had a new dress for dances," said Jeanine, her daughter. "Mom would say, 'Here's three dresses. I'm sure you'll like one of them.' And of course I got to keep the other two anyway."

It was Dottie's joy to grow *Hospitality Hostess Service* and train women to earn a good living, By helping people when they moved to a new area, she helped the merchants find new clients. It wasn't just win-win. It was win- win- and WIN. Everyone connected with Dottie won.

Building *Hospitality Hostess Service* is where Dottie gained the experience that would blast her into fame almost a decade later. It would be ten years after she got her big break at the paper until she wrote her first book. In that time, Dottie learned the ropes of selling. Ironically, it is the thing she talked to me about the least. She mostly mentioned the milestones in her life, the turning points, the opportunities like the soda fountain, the people who influenced her. She was always delighted to be helping someone with a great idea or a challenge they were facing at that moment. She lives in the now.

The Friendly Words

The phone was very important in Dottie's era. "Perhaps your telephone is diamond studded," she said. "It's so fast, so inexpensive, so satisfying." In one of her newsletters, Dottie is pictured in a cartoon drawing with Jack Schwartz, a famous salesman and author of the era. In a question and answer volley across the page from each other,

Jack said, "Tell me Dottie...where does new business go?"

Dottie: "It always goes where it's invited Jack. But where does new business stay? "

Jack: "New business like old business, stays where it is appreciated."

Hospitality Newsletter

"Goodwill is priceless. Goodwill is my business."
Dottie Walters

Dottie constantly encouraged both sides of her team. She began a monthly newsletter containing an inspirational message. During the recession of 1958 she wrote, "Please don't be discouraged at the little dullness of business. The constant growth of our country will increase the trade of all who steadily stand ready for it." She

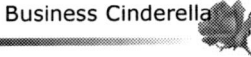

always personalized the newsletters. At the bottom she wrote, "God loves you and so does…Dottie." And she did.

Dottie was smart. She shared the raving letters she received from very satisfied clients in her newsletters and passed along advice from the best of the best. With the monthly mailing and billings, she sent out a newsletter filled with great tips, and upbeat advice. By providing not only a service, but something entertaining and useful, the monthly bill must've seemed quite enjoyable to pay!

Even a grumpy sponsor who'd been complaining that Dottie wasn't getting him results, was a convert. Dottie said, "The truth was his negative attitude scared his customers away." The man came to visit her the day after she had sent out one of her newsletters. Dottie thought he'd come to withdraw his account. But that wasn't the reason. He came to tell Dottie, "That newsletter really made me stop and think." Dottie could sweeten even the most bitter of people.

Dottie also took on the responsibility of the *Hospitality Hostess* to find ways to continue to pay for their home. She wanted to be able to work as much as possible from home because she had young children to raise. By now, she had four children, Robert, Michael, Jeanine, and Lilly. By the time she sold the business ten years later, it had grown to employ 30 hostesses. "My one humble talent kept mushrooming," she said." Dottie started right in Baldwin Park. "I started where I was planted," she said. "A lot of people give up and say, 'I'm not in the right area, I don't have a car.' They use any excuse. People can spend their whole lives doing that. They are looking in the wrong place. When opportunity comes, grab it." Dottie knows. You have to look inside for your success.

Today, Dottie is still a gracious hostess. She always asks what the other person needs, makes sure they are comfortable, and provides stimulating conversation and ideas to think about.

A sign goes up in San Diego for Dottie's
Hospitality Hostess Service

Ask For What You Deserve

When you start building strong, solid relationships with people, opportunity loves to show up. While Dottie was speaking at a Kiwanis luncheon, a man came up to Dottie after her talk on customer service. The man was Harold Harris of the elegant Harris Departments stores throughout Southern California. He was having a Christmas luncheon for his employees where they would be getting awards. Mr. Harris wanted Dottie to give her talk and asked how much her fee was. Dottie asked him if all the personnel would be at one luncheon or if it would be four separate luncheons. Mr. Harris said he was offering $100. Dottie said, "I took a deep breath and said, 'Mr. Harris. I accept your offer of $100 each for your four store joint luncheon.' Harris laughed out loud and told her, "Dottie, you are not dumb." We know that!

As Dottie spoke and became better known and more successful in her own business, she looked for ways to improve both herself and her business. She again looked to her favorite place...the library. It had a big influence on the next chapter of her life...her first book.

CHAPTER 7
Her First Book

Laura Webb, one of Dottie's
Hospitality Hostesses helps celebrate
Dottie's first book

The Nonexistent Book

"I wanted to read books about women in sales, because I was just starting out," said Dottie. "I asked the librarian to help me. She couldn't find a book on that topic and had checked with all the other libraries, first within the county, and then the state. She said, 'There aren't any. There's nothing for women.' And I said, "None?" At that moment an image flashed into Dottie's mind. Where others saw lack, Dottie saw great opportunity.

Never Underestimate the Selling Power of THIS Woman

Dottie used her great tool of visualization. She is a master at it. "That night I walked back to the books on business," she said. "I had read everything they had there. Then I saw it. I saw my book! I saw the color. I saw my picture on the front. I saw the title, *Never Underestimate the Selling Power of a Woman*. I saw the whole thing. I started working on the book. I submitted it to 26 different publishers who all turned it down. They said there were no women in sales in America. I thought, 'None in the whole country?' Well I knew that was wrong because there were women who worked in sales in department stores and in many places. I went ahead and finished the book. Then I got the chance to hear Dr. Norman Vincent Peale speak."

Her Second Big Break: The Meeting With Doctor Peale

Dottie went to hear Dr. Peale in person. He was speaking in Pasadena, California. In order to get to the event, she traded babysitting services with a neighbor for the use of her car. Dottie just had her first business cards printed and thought, "What if I could give him the first one that anyone ever got, the first one out of the little box?" Dottie waited in the long line to see Dr. Peale after his talk. When she got up to him, she had the card in her hand. Suddenly, she got afraid and thought, "What if he turns it down? What if he pushes it away? Oh, that will break my heart. I don't want to cry in front of him. What am I going to do?" But instead, Dr. Peale told her, "What is that in your hand, dear?" Dottie remembers fondly. "Oh, he was such a loving man! I told him that I had started my business on foot, pushing the babies in a stroller with a wheel that kept coming off, with cardboard in my shoes." Dottie told Dr. Peale that these were her very first business cards and she wanted him to have the first one, then held it out to him. He noticed the gesture and said, "Is that the card in your hand? May I have it?" When Dottie said, "Yes," he reached out and took the card from her. Then he did something that Dottie suggests every man does when a woman gives you her business card. "He put it in the pocket by his heart! Do you think that a woman didn't notice that?" Dottie exclaimed. "Of course I noticed it. Every woman does! I was just overwhelmed to think that he would offer that loving gesture to me! He said, 'We'll be in touch.' Wasn't that beautiful?"

Cover Girl

Many beautiful and exciting things started happening in Dottie's life. Dr. Peale called her. "I about dropped the phone!" she said. "Is it really you?" He said, "Yes, I'm telling your story every time I speak. We want to do a story about you in *Guidepost Magazine*."

Dottie was thrilled and said, "Oh. Dr. Peale! Yes, I'd be honored to be in *Guidepost*." Dr. Peale arranged to send a reporter out to interview her. The reporter wanted to call the article, "What Can One Housewife Do?" The whole issue of *Guidepost* was on that theme because at that time many people were having financial troubles. *Guidepost* wanted to inspire others with what this feisty housewife accomplished. She made her first cover in April of 1959. Dottie was a subscriber to *Guidepost* and loved it because she said it was "always so full of positive thoughts. It's a wonderful magazine and it's still being published."

Guideposts

How a woman found her way to fame and fortune by changing her own attitude from "I Can't Do Anything" to "I Will do something"

This inspiring true story shows how a woman can use the "power within" to rise above any difficulties.

Reprinted from and Under Copyright By
GUIDEPOSTS MAGAZINE
Carmel, N. Y.

Dottie made the cover of *Guidepost* magazine!

During the interview with *Guidepost,* Dottie noticed the last question the reporter asked her was a very good one for an interviewer. The reporter asked Dottie what was she working on next. Dottie told her about the book she was writing about women in sales.

Dr. Peale called back and said, "Dottie, I use your story every time I speak. I mention that you are working on the book. Everybody wants to buy it. Who is your publisher?" Dottie had to reply, "Oh, Dr. Peale, I don't have one yet." She told him about the number of publishers that had turned her down, saying that there are no women in sales in America. Dr. Peale laughed. Dottie described his voice as sounding like bells, just like his name. Dr. Peale said, "They told you there were no women in sales in all of America? Well, you and I both know that that's not true!" That warmed Dottie's heart. "The spirit of kindness," she called him. Dr. Peale told her he was going to see his publisher, Prentice-Hall, the next day and he would take along a stack of *Guideposts* with Dottie's picture on the front. Prentice-Hall called Dottie and asked her to send the manuscript. When Dr. Peale called Dottie back he said, "Dottie, my publisher is going to publish it. They have already sold out the entire first edition to Tupperware!"

Dottie speaks of that opportunity. "You see, people didn't have all the information. The people who were publishing books were thinking of people who sold big things - large buildings or real estate. They thought there wasn't enough interest to sell books on teaching business skills like selling to women. That just wasn't true. There were women in many fields, or wanted to be." Once Tupperware bought her book, then Amway bought it. The other direct sales companies followed. With her enormous success, they wanted Dottie to be at their meetings as the author of the book. They each bought several thousand copies. That's when she started speaking to all those direct sales companies. Her fame grew.

Dottie's book was a hit right from the start! Her title, *Never Underestimate the Selling Power of a Woman,* was a self-fulfilling prophecy. Those first publishers who rejected her book sure *did* underestimate Dottie and the book. It was a best seller and is still being published today. Prentice-Hall took everything except for one chapter. The chapter was on how men should sell to women. Dottie felt that she couldn't leave the men out of her story. It was important to her to include them too. Her instincts were right on. She had just written the first book for women is sales in the world.

CHAPTER 8
More Fame

The Seven Secrets
of Selling To Women

"Lift people up and they will back you up."
Dottie Walters

Her next opportunity didn't take long to manifest. Dottie looked at the chapter her publisher returned. In the very same mail she got a postcard from a company down in Texas starting a new business making "talking" books - the first audio books. They wondered if she had anything that would make a good topic for an audio book. Bingo! She thought of her unused chapter. Here was the perfect solution!

Dottie gave them the name of the chapter, *"The Seven Secrets of Selling to Women,"* the same title she had given that chapter in her book that Prentice-Hall had left out. The audio company called her back and said, "Yes, we want to use it for an album. We will do a geometric design for the cover." Dottie wasn't too thrilled with the cover idea so she set out to find a place to do the recording, and recorded it herself.

Dottie whispering the seven secrets

Dottie had a friend whose husband had a good-looking head of hair, especially from the back. Dottie asked her friend if she'd bring her well-coifed husband over and let her take his picture. Dottie had the man sit on the piano bench because there was a particular look she was going for. "I wanted it to appear like I was giving him the special *Seven Secrets of Selling to Women*," she said. Facing forward with her hand over her mouth, Dottie appeared to be whispering in his ear. That would also show the handsome back of his head. Dottie's friend agreed and helped her with the photo. That's the man with Dottie on the cover of that album above.

The audio company never had time to send Dottie the geometric design. She finished it in a week! When they saw it, they loved it and made it into her first audio album. Dottie was astonished at who bought most of those albums. It was the US Navy! "I got letters from all those sailors. They were playing them on board! I was glad, but I think they were thinking of a different kind of selling! Even so, the same principles of being a loving person, and not a mean person is what the "Seven Secrets" were all about."

Dottie had something in common with these great women!

Seven Roses

Dottie had superb ideas and her timing was so great, but she also did a lot of research and had all that background from reading about successful people. Women were just beginning to come into their own. Her audio album became very popular. She put a border of roses down the left-hand side of the cover photograph. Dottie was curious where we got the idea of the rose being connected to love. She researched this and said, "It was Venus. Venus used to come down and visit men in ancient Rome. Venus had Cupid sit out on the front stoop giving out roses. Notice the statue of Cupid always says, 'Shush!' with his finger up to his mouth. He is saying, 'Be quiet. Love is going on here!" Dottie thought it was an interesting story. Inside her audio book, she had seven sections, each one with a picture of a rose on it. "That album was quite a hit. I sold thousands of them." Over ten thousand to be exact!

To Tell the Truth or Not

Another big break was on the horizon for Dottie - a chance to appear before millions of people. Her career was soaring. Dr. Peale called her with the following news. "Now that we have the book going," he said, "have you ever been on a television show?" She had not. Dr. Peale told her he would be in touch and worked a little of his magic. "The first thing I know," Dottie said, "I'm getting a call from a show called *To Tell the Truth*." This was a very popular TV program of the 1950s and 60s. Three people came out on stage and the celebrity panel had to guess who was the real person and who was bluffing. They choose someone with a unique occupation or someone who had done something noteworthy. Dottie fit both categories. The celebrities asked the panelists questions that usually had yes or no answers. The other two contestants looked very much like Dottie – her age and coloring - until they opened their mouths.

The first lady was from the Bronx with a real strong Bronx accent. The next lady said, "I'm the real Dottie Walters and I'm the author of the book." That woman came from the South, dressed in a neat white suit, and white gloves. With her southern accent she stated that she had a ladies finishing school where she taught students to be very polite and ladylike. They announced the third lady (who was the real Dottie), "Now we have the girl from the chicken ranching town of Baldwin Park, California. She's claiming to be the true author of *Never Underestimate the Selling Power of a Woman.*" Dottie said, "Yes, I come from the chicken ranching town of Baldwin Park, and I *am* the real Dottie Walters." "Everyone laughed! Dottie said. "The audience went into hysterics. They all thought that it couldn't be me, because how could you make a living in a chicken ranching town?"

The ladies were asked questions and they each had to answer them. The last question was, "Who was the first great advertising salesman?" Dottie noted said they said "man" referring again to her need for her timely book on women in sales. She thought that perhaps they may have even given the other two ladies bogus answers to say because they responded with names such as "Ogilvy" a man well known in the field of advertising at the time. When they asked Dottie the same question, she replied confidently, "Ladies, I'm sorry, but you're wrong. You see it was my great friend of the mind, Benjamin Franklin." As Dottie explained why it was Franklin, a booming voice came from the speaker above saying, "Ladies and Gentleman. We have a winner! Dottie Walters from the chicken ranching town of Baldwin Park!" Dottie was given money to appear on the television show. She didn't remember the amount but said it felt like a huge sum to her and her husband, Bob, who came along to New York to see his wife on the TV Show.

When Dottie and Bob returned to Baldwin Park, the Chamber of Commerce had a banquet to welcome their successful daughter home. No more would she ever have to wear cardboard in her shoes in this town. She was now famous.

**Dottie at one of the many ribbon cutting
events she attended in California**

Part of a proclamation from the Mayor of Baldwin Park read:

WHEREAS; our "daughter" Dottie Walters began a business here in Baldwin Park fourteen (14) years ago without even a car, pushing her babies before her in a stroller; and WHEREAS; Dottie Walters has now written a book about business entitled, THE SELLING POWER OF A WOMAN in order to help others find opportunity...

It went on to name November 13, 1962, Dottie Walters Day.

Dottie was in *Who's Who In American Women*, on countless radio shows, TV programs and was even on the program on American Airlines.

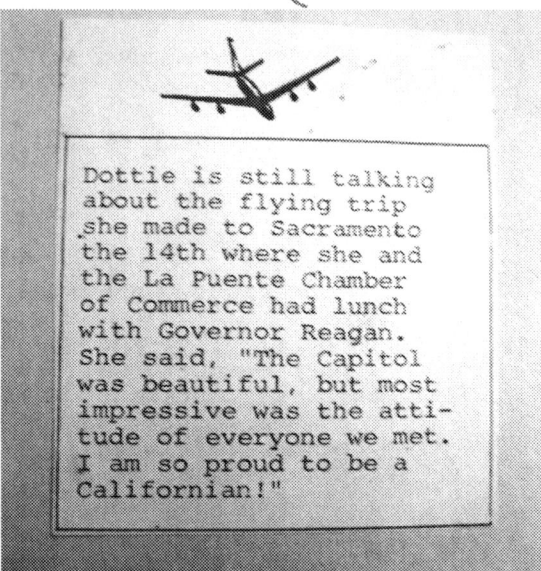

Dottie is still talking about the flying trip she made to Sacramento the 14th where she and the La Puente Chamber of Commerce had lunch with Governor Reagan. She said, "The Capitol was beautiful, but most impressive was the attitude of everyone we met. I am so proud to be a Californian!"

Dottie was invited to dine with Governor Reagan

Communication is basically a transfer of information from one person to another. Dottie was a master at it. Once she flew up to Sacramento to have lunch with Governor Ronald Reagan. Can you imagine the two great communicators dining together?

CHAPTER 9
The View From the Top of the Speaking World

Her Catapult to the Conventions

*'It has been said that our eyes are the windows of our soul.
If this is true then surely our mouth is the broadcasting station."*
Dottie Walters

Dottie began speaking for two reasons, she had a message and she had a book. And she had the outstanding ability to deliver it. She began her journey of inspiring hundreds of thousands of people with that message. Remember this woman was trained by the likes of Einstein, Franklin, Edison, and Shakespeare.

A lady who was head of one of the direct sales companies went to a bookstore and saw Dottie's book on display. She called Dottie to come and speak to them. This company put on sales seminars for their people all over the country. Dottie did dozens of talks for them.

The direct sales companies bought Dottie's book for every person that worked for them. It was a time when direct sales companies were springing up everywhere. They wanted Dottie to tell her story at their conventions. "That was the beginning of my speaking all over the world," she says.

Back then, even though women were selling, Dottie inspired countless women with a new idea - that women were capable of the sales that they had been doing all along! Women were ready to take their place in the world as saleswomen.

Speaking of Dottie

*"Every salesperson has to surmount obstacles
and get up when she is knocked down."*
Dottie Walters

"The book opened my career for speaking," Dottie said. The first time Dottie went out speaking to groups larger than the local service clubs, she had to learn professional speaking skills. Here's how she did it. "I told my own story of how I wouldn't stay down and how I wasn't going to lose the house," she said. "I had a goal – to keep our home. I think setting a goal is very important. When people see that you keep your word, that you do what you say you'll do, and that you that have ideas - everybody likes someone with ideas - then opportunity starts knocking at your door. When it starts knocking, for goodness sake, open it!" Dottie instinctively knew a secret - once you let opportunity in, even more doors will open for you!

"I have learned it's not the size of the audience that matters, for I have spoken to as few as ten and as many as 5,000 for the Amway Corporation. I find inspiration for my writing and speaking in reading the Great Ideas of Mankind."

Because of Dottie's charm, and her great ability as a story teller (reading all those books helped!) audiences loved her. Each time she spoke, she would get several deals and future speaking engagements. Every event had publicity connected with it, which in turn garnered more calls to Dottie for additional speaking. It exploded.

The Soft Sell

"The greatest gift you can give to anyone is your attention."
Dottie Walters

Two selling cultures were merging. A newspaper article showed a man holding a bullwhip. Dottie stood next to the man, offering up a red rose and her smile. It could have been a photo statement for the whole era.

Dottie entered a world where women were just coming into their own. It wasn't an easy transition but Dottie softened the blow She could walk between the worlds of women and men with equal ease. She was sharp and determined enough to never give up until she had completed her task - to show women how to break into the business game that men had been playing. "Employed women today are a permanent reality," she said. "We are not a hangover from world wars or a temporary economic expansion."

Dottie started to speak around the country, and then the world about this newfangled idea – women in sales! She had few problems with her audiences because of her warmth and wit. It didn't hurt that she was a very attractive woman, described as "tall, slender, with red-gold hair and wide blue eyes."

In Dallas, Dottie told her audience, "If there's one thing a woman is without anything contrived, it is a persuader. Ever since Eve sold Adam that produce item." A headline said, "How a man can sell a women?" Sounds like slavery to me but it sold papers, magazines and speeches. Another headline read, "7 Secrets for Men – How to beat women at their own game." This one showed a photo of a salesman pointing out the practical side of a pitcher to a woman who is trying to mentally match the color to her dining room draperies. Dottie "got" the differences between the sexes and could explain them humorously, strategically and accurately. "Men customers take things at their face value; women customers want PROOF," she said.

"I belong to a club of women sales executives started by a gal named EVE who did a pretty good selling job to a man named Adam, " Dottie said. "Since then, there have been a lot of members – such as Cleopatra, Sarah Bernhardt, Carrie Nation, Harriet Beecher Stowe."

Dottie told another story that illustrates the way women sell, "A man afraid of a dog will say, 'nice doggy' – and all the while he is looking around for a rock to throw. A woman will say, 'nice doggy' and keep on saying it until she's convinced the dog that he really is nice." She got to the essence of why people buy. Encyclopedias were not mere books to her, but "success insurance!"

"There is no pushiness in selling; you are there to help, to serve, to brighten each and every woman's life. The selling power is already within you," she said. "In order to sell, you must first serve. If you feel someone is beneath you, you can never serve him."

"I don't think to myself, 'I have to sell this account. I need the money," she said. 'Instead, I say, 'How can I help his business?' Step into your prospects shoes so completely that you leave yourself behind. Get into step with your customer. You must do the fitting in, not him. Successful selling is a difference in perspective. Say, 'Tell me about it.' And write down all the information."

"Don't underestimate women," Dottie said. "Men make the mistake of trying to understand women. Quit that stuff, won't you? It's our role to be understanding. It's your role to be appreciative." Dottie charmed men. She became a hero to women.

A Giving Voice

When Dottie worked briefly at the Los Angeles Times, she noticed that a top saleswoman closed her eyes to shut out the outer world when she made her sales calls. "She taught me a big lesson," said Dottie. "How much a saleswoman can do with her voice. Your tone of voice can also give you away. Keep it low and your words slow and controlled."

What it Means to Sell

Her number one rule of selling to women? *Agree with them.* Some of the teasers listed on her first book were, "Learn who was first saleswoman in history," and "Learn how you can turn a lion into a lamb." The rest of her brilliant advice is in her book.

Here is Dottie's demonstration of how to sell toys. "Let's say your customer has picked up a stuffed toy dog. 'Hi there you cute little fellow. Sit up! Atta Boy. Fido!' You say to the toy puppy. Your customer grins. 'He'll be lonesome without company,' you say. 'Here's his mother over here. And daddy has a pipe and slippers.'" Dottie went on to sell the whole family and their cousins! Only Dottie could do that.

"You are selling status, prestige, adoration, popularity, rest, youth, security, and even good judgment to people. The way you handle your product is very important. If you show that you admire and respect your item, your customer will too," she said.

"If you lose your special enthusiasm, you can't sell. People prefer doing business with cheerful enthusiastic people, for your attitude rubs off on them."

The inspiration for the title of her book came from Mona Ling, a nationally recognized telephone sales consultant who Dottie deeply respected. Mona said, "Never underestimate the selling power of a woman. Selling is easy and natural for women." Dottie agreed completely.

Dottie's book was a hit among men sharp enough to see what she had done. Jack Schwartz wrote her, "You are now in the first leg of world-wide fame and needless to say, I'll be cheering you all the way." Napoleon Hill wrote, "Congratulations. You've made the big league." He thanked her for the autographed copy and said, "I consider it a masterpiece." Norman Vincent Peale said, "I admire Dottie's spirit and the tenacity with which she has kept her 'dream' in mind and worked it until it became a reality," The accolades continued for decades.

The Selling Power of Women was the first book by a woman to make *Success Unlimited* magazine in August 1976. Joan Talmage Weiss of *Success Unlimited* wrote, "If you knew your husband's business was about to fail, what would you do? Would you just quit? Or would you be a Dottie Walters?"

What Do Women Want

*"Going the extra mile means giving your customers
and your company 13 eggs to the dozen."*
Dottie Walters

So, what *do* women really want? "They want something to make their life easier, or more pleasant, or more interesting. They want a bargain," said Dottie.

Dottie kept inspiration close and carried a yellowed card in her purse, "7 Rules I use in closing the sale" by Frank Bettger. She read it whenever she had a minute. Bettger's first rule? *Attention.*

You might have thought Dottie could read minds. She knew how to pay attention and became an expert at looking for the "clues" of what someone wanted. What "I can read your face" actually meant was, "Watch his face for an expression change, which indicates his feelings," she said. Dottie understood the basis of sales. "You have to know you've got what they need, and you have to see that they get it."

Of her book she said, "Perhaps the story of my struggles can be helpful to other women who have to make their way in the world. I sincerely believe that selling is easier for women than for men. We have an inborn ability – the womanly art of persuasion. It is part of our very nature to be motherly, warm and concerned for others."

Crumpled No More

"When you serve people you step into a limelight, which carries a responsibility to be womanly and gracious."
Dottie Walters

Once Dottie went to see a man. He took her business card and threw it in the wastebasket. Yes, at first she was appalled and could have reacted in kind. "Instead, I lowered my voice, leaned toward him and said very slowly and sadly, 'I am so surprised to see you do that. I am shocked at a man with your wonderful reputation and responsible position treating anyone, even someone as lowly as I like this." The man stared at Dottie, then let out his breath, retrieved her card and asked her to forgive him. Her card went respectfully where it belonged, into his wallet.

"Each customer no matter how odd or difficult – presents a lesson to be learned," she said. "Each successful saleswoman I know, has in some way tapped the unlimited power of God's love, for the womanly art of persuasion is in our hearts and has been there all along. We must only learn how to *use* this gift. The higher art of selling is service. When we are really serving others, we are selling in the highest form."

Dottie spoke at the Tupperware conventions. "Say to yourself, 'I want to serve these people,' she told them. "If you truly feel this way, you won't have time to be bashful or self-conscious." At the time the party plan like Tupperware's was very popular. "It's success lies in the fact that it combines a social element with the commercial one." Dottie said. She also highly respected Avon's saleswomen.

But Dottie never forgot her priorities. She used to tell Bob when he'd come and get her at the airport (he was always there when she got back) 'You know, that's the best part of the trip. To come back and find you here waiting for me!"

Bob Walters on one of his beloved horses

The Solution is at Hand, The Dottie Walters Story

Bob was extremely proud of Dottie and what she was accomplishing. He did everything he could to help. It became a business they both worked on together. But Bob was also very busy on his own. He taught swimming and gave merit badges to the local boy scouts at their large pool at the ranch. "He loved doing that," Dottie said. Bob was an avid horseman and did some volunteer work for the mounted sheriff's search and rescue when someone was lost in the mountains behind their home. Jeanine said. "He knew all the sheriffs. Everyone called him "Cowboy Bob." Dottie said that Bob loved riding horses. Sometimes he'd go riding all weekend with his friends. He was worried that might upset Dottie. She told him, "Honey, if it makes you happy, you do it." Then she asked Bob, 'What do you need? Lunches packed?" "If you love someone, you want them to be happy," she said.

Dottie and Bob, always in love.

"He was instrumental and always at her side," said Joe Kessler, a friend. "Bob always gave her encouragement. Dottie was very much in love with him. He was a wonderful man - big in heart and stature. The two of them were wonderful together." With Bob's support and her determination, Dottie's business continued to evolve. The next opportunity was waiting in the wings for Dottie.

CHAPTER 10
Bureaus and Sharing Ideas

The Queen of Speakers Bureaus

Sometimes when Dottie spoke, people asked her if she knew of a speaker who could talk on a particular subject. Since she was on the speaking circuit, she got to know the other speakers and their specialties. Dottie often could recommend someone for a particular talk. "I thought that maybe this is another opportunity knocking on my door," she said. "Maybe I need to start a speaker's bureau. So I did."

Walters International Speakers Bureau was born. It grew to the one of the largest bureaus in the world, representing over 24,000 speakers. The bureau also publishes a directory of all the speaker bureaus around the globe. Many bureaus specialize. For example, there are a few that only book athletes. Dottie recommends that speakers research each bureau. "If you're a speaker who is an athlete, then you want to call that bureau, but if you're not an athlete, don't call them! They're going to say 'No,' because that's not what they do. They specialize with athletes who are speakers."

NSA Great Los Angeles Chapter
Founded in 1984 by Dottie Walters

Dottie was the founder of the NSA Greater Los Angeles Chapter and to this day is revered in the organization. She had a lot to offer the group. NSA trains speakers to present themselves professionally. In the early years there was a great deal of enthusiasm. "What amazed me was how willing the speakers were to help each other and come up with innovative ideas," said Connie Yambert, NSA member. It started from a need and an idea - the recipe Dottie was always good at.

NSA, LA started with about twenty people around a dinner table to talk about beginning the chapter. The table is always a good place to get to know people and Dottie used it effectively. NSA National at the time only had about 60 members, so her new group increased NSA by a full third. It was a very significant contribution to the world of speaking. Originally, people came from both Los Angeles and Orange counties. Once they tried alternating between LA and OC but found the OC people came to the OC meetings and the LA people came to the LA meetings. That wasn't going to work! So they changed it to the Greater Los Angeles Chapter of NSA to encompass both groups and left it at that.

At those early meetings, Dottie talked about the eight facets to being a professional speaker. She gave a lot of insightful info about little things as well as big things, like how to do a one sheet and how to write a book. Dottie took it even further and told speakers how to hold the book and how to love it so that the audience loves it as well.

Connie Yambert, said, "Once we were speaking at a convention in Chicago and the people who put on the convention asked if we would room together, which we did. Dottie was on the phone all night because she had international business to do. I thought, "The woman never sleeps!"

Nan Pratt, owner of Standing Ovations Speakers Bureau, who was involved from the beginning said, "I saw speakers range from $1,000 to $50,000 per speech and up. I was invited to serve because of Dottie's encouragement. Dottie got me to join. I'm type A. Dottie is a secret Type A. She gives me plenty of ideas. Dottie would say 'Why don't we start this and try this for NSA?'

She thought NSA would help me have a more rounded understanding."

Dottie stayed active for quite awhile in NSA but then she got busy with her next projects, her magazine and bureau. "I think she outgrew us," said Connie. "She was so far advanced. She was also active on the national chapter as well. We always revered her as the founder."

In 2004 Dottie was awarded a Lifetime Achievement Award by NSA. It is one of her most treasured awards. "Sometimes something that doesn't seem that important at the time because of all the other things that were going on at that time too, is something that later, really made a difference," Dottie said.

Then Dottie noticed yet another missing link in the speaking world. There was no organization for Speakers Bureau owners. Leave it to Dottie. She organized the first one.

Speaker Bureaus Unite

Two years after starting the powerful new NSA chapter, Dottie saw the need for another group. She had been very active in NSA for years. It was at the NSA Greater LA meetings that Dottie realized there needed to be a separate organization for speaker's bureaus. Up to that point the only place to gather had been at the annual conventions. However, the conventions didn't lend themselves very well for bureaus to network and address the important issues that they were facing. All speakers' bureaus vary. Some do training, some focus on certain types of speakers. There was no organizing force until Dottie. The IASB, International Association of Speakers Bureaus, originally called IGAB, the International Group of Associations and Bureaus, was born.

Joe Kessler who owns a speakers bureau was at that very first meeting held in Boston. He describes what it was like. "They all got in the room and stood around with their arms folded, eyeing each other with great suspicion." "Joe didn't think anyone would get out of the room without there being blood shed." Jim Montoya current Executive VP said, "Dottie softened that atmosphere. She had all the key players there to make it a reality. John Palmer was there." Years later, Dottie would receive the *John Palmer Award* for outstanding service to the speaking industry.

"Dottie held some meetings at her home. Everyone was delightful," said Kessler. "She sold ads for her column to build up her sales capabilities. It was extremely difficult in those days to get anybody's attention if you were a woman. She was a pioneer." She was highly respected by her peers and that's one of the reasons people were willing to follow her ideas. The other reason is that they were great ideas."

People back then were not willing to share how they built their business or gave much help to each other. Dottie had a huge influence on changing that behavior. She conducted her business a new way and got terrific results, which she willingly shared with others. Kessler said, "I find that most of those in the business had camaraderie and high energy level, because entrepreneurs were more unusual in those days. Today you have a lot more tools. The telephone was the only tool you had back then. My first computer cost $35,000 to $40,000." Again Dottie used what she had – what was at hand.

Today when members come together in IASB, they openly share ideas. That's good business. "Conventions are like big family reunions. Bureaus usually operate in isolation," said Jim Montoya. "Here they come together face to face. It used to be downright cutthroat between bureaus. Early on there were no rules. That was the driving force for Dottie. She saw that if people would come together and work together, they could benefit. It worked. It took time, but it worked."

Now IASB is in its 20th year. Shana Stillman. President of the Washington Speakers Bureau, the largest in the country, was at the 2005 convention. She works with the likes of Colin Powell and Rudy Giuliani. They co-broker with other bureaus. If one gets a request for someone who is signed with another bureau, they'll work out a deal and split the commissions. They both benefit. Shana said that they had fewer problems when they worked with bureaus that were members of IASB and that beginning June 1st, the Washington Speakers Bureau would only co-broker with members of IASB. It sent shock waves throughout the speaking world. IASB had 100 members at the time of Shana's bold statement. Since then, IASB grew by 30 additional members.

The IASB stresses the importance of conducting businesses in an ethical manner. Bureaus have to sign an agreement to operate ethically. "What is even more meaningful to me," said Montoya, "is that they (The Washington Speakers Bureau) feel that this is so important to this industry that they were willing to take that stand. That spoke volumes. Dottie did see the vision and cleaned up the business to make it good for everyone. I know without question that this organization has been a driving force in changing the speaking industry for the better."

Kessler said, "I was an independent speakers bureau. Dottie called and said I should definitely join. It was a new group she had put together. It was good to meet with competition and get insights into mindsets of people in the business. When you get involved with your competition you can share concerns and war stories."

What Dottie accomplished in bringing together the speaker's bureaus was the same thing she did with the *Hospitality Hostess*

Service. She brought people together who could benefit by being with each other.

Sharing Ideas

Out of her bureau grew *Sharing Ideas*, Dottie's magazine that goes to thousands of subscribers from speakers, to event planners, to the systems that support them, like designers and CD manufacturers. Many recognizable and famous names grace the cover from Jack Canfield to Dan Kennedy and Les Brown. It is the leading magazine of the speaking industry.

The *Sharing Ideas* magazine has been published for almost three decades. Dottie is especially pleased to hear stories of subscribers who go outside to get their mail, grab their issue of *Sharing Ideas* and sit on the steps until they have read the whole magazine. That gives her immense pleasure.

A consulting business was the next business that grew out of her reputation. Dottie has a real knack for passing along advice and helping to build successful business people. Her insights on a person's business and the next steps to take towards greater success become so apparent after talking with her that you wonder why you hadn't thought of that yourself! It's a natural talent of hers. People who have consulted with Dottie are some of the most famous of household names.

Speaking Advice

For speakers out there who want to get booked, here's is a quick piece of free advice from Dottie. You might want to follow her advice; she has booked thousands of speakers all over the world.

"Get your kit ready," she says. "You have got to have a presentation folder with the name of your talk in bright colors across the top. Make it big enough so it can be seen across the room. Add your photo. It has to look good. Maybe use a full-length photo. Across the bottom, put your name. The event planners use your presentation folder along with the information you have inside to consider booking you. They may be considering two or three other speakers, so it has to look great because it's going to be looked at by the board of directors of the association putting on the convention. They are considering you against several other speakers. We choose to send you because you are what they are looking for." Dottie serves the event planners and their requests. She says, "If that is you and your topic, that is how you get booked."

One particular pet peeve of Dottie's is when a speaker calls her and tells her they can speak on any topic. She doesn't like that nor does she like it when speakers ask her what the "hot" topic is right now. She wants experts. You must talk on what you already know. That's what bonds you to people.

Another thing that ticks her off is when someone calls and offers her a "bonus" if they will book them over other speakers. If a speaker was ever rude or tried to bribe her – watch out! Dottie would never compromise her integrity that way. All her speakers are important. Her job was to match speakers and their topics and expertise, to the particular event they were requested for. She does this to give the best value to the meeting planners. Then they will want to use Walters Speakers Bureau again because of the great results she gave them. Dottie nurtured that relationship to the benefit of all her speakers.

One other taboo of speakers sent out by her bureau was if a speaker took the job, then solicited "extra" business out of that event. Because the bureau got them the job, all leads from that job should go back to the bureau. Word gets around to all the bureaus when speakers do this and it destroys the speaker's credibility with the bureaus. Trust is very important to Dottie. It tells who you are.

Here are the Traits Dottie Feels a Speaker Should Have

*"If we can only love people enough,
we will know how to deal with them."*
Dottie Walters

Her number one trait to be a speaker? "I think they should have visualization," she says. "The first time I ever spoke to an audience of about 5,000 people, it was in a huge auditorium. There were several balconies of people. I arrived there in the daytime and walked out on the stage and thought, 'I won't be nervous, I'll be all right.' Another speaker backstage said to me, 'You know, I always picture them naked. Then I can stand there and just laugh at them. They're all boney and fat and ugly.' I thought to myself, 'I don't like that idea. I'll think of something, but I won't do that!"

"Instead, I'm going to visualize that they are all my children, like the whole auditorium is filled with my children! I'm going to walk out there with my hands out to the audience, palms out, starting over here, looking all over the auditorium. I'm going to think at them, 'Here I am. I'm the one you've been waiting for!" With that thought in her head and heart when she went on stage, Dottie's audience gave her two standing ovations during her talk, and another huge one at the end. She was visualizing in a way that touched the hearts of people. She could always reach her audiences because of her love for them. They felt it and connected with her.

Visualize Solutions

Dottie explains why she tells stories when a question is asked of her. "You can tell something you want people to learn by telling them a story, or writing a poem. If they can see the picture that's in your mind transferred to their mind, then that's being a great speaker, or being a great writer too. When you read a book you are communicating with that author," she said. Through our stories we can touch people throughout time as an author does.

"Most of the time when we fail to use our will power, it's because our imagination hasn't given us a clear picture of just what we want. Hold that picture steadfastly," she said. "Before going to sleep every night, visualize it in your mind."

A lady who lives in Canada told Dottie, "You mean to tell me that all the great people you quoted here, wrote their books for you? That's ridiculous!" Dottie replied, "Who do you think they wrote them for? They wrote them for us and for everyone in this room who ever needs some help, who ever needs inspiration! That's in spirit – inspiration!"

Her Brilliant Connection

"I believe all authors write for the listening heart."
Dottie Walters

This amazing story that illustrates the way Dottie connects to people when she speaks. A lady came down from the top balcony and said to Dottie, "I almost didn't stay because I thought, 'Oh, another dumb woman speaker." Dottie gently asked her, "You don't like women speakers?" The lady said, "No I don't!" Dottie took her hand and said, "You know, we women have got to help each other. Don't forget that." The woman said, "Well, it's when they put that pink spotlight on you that I decided to stay." Dottie told me, "There was no spotlight! The house lights were up. Isn't that amazing? She saw the love that I was projecting!" Dottie had a loving thought. That's what the audience felt and connected with.

"Any speaker can do the same," Dottie said. "Figure your own thing that you are thinking at them. They will see it and feel it. I think that is what actors do. You believe that they were the bad guy or the good guy, because they are an actor and that's what they're visualizing."

After we'd attend some event with one or usually several speakers, Dottie gave me wonderful lessons on speaking professionally. She'd talk to me and analyze the speech. Then she'd discuss what she liked about the speech and the presentation and what could be improved upon.

Dottie told me to give a gift to the person who introduces you. She always gives a little gift to the introducer, usually a book. Not only is it a gesture of kindness and good taste, but this creates an unspoken contract to deliver the introduction for the speaker as given. Often times the introducer would go on and on. That drove Dottie nuts. Whether it was for her speech or when she listened to someone else, she wanted to get right to the main course.

"Objections are actually questions in reverse."
Dottie Walters

Not everybody has agreed with what Dottie has said when she's spoken. Every speaker has to learn how to handle this. When someone puts themselves in the public arena, they are in the spotlight. It's natural for some people to find something they don't agree with. Dottie didn't concern herself with this. She accepted it as a worthwhile risk for those willing to deliver a valuable message. If somebody wanted to argue a point with Dottie when she was speaking she said, "I try to give them an out without there being a fight over it. I say, 'That's an interesting angle. Would you tell us more about it?' And of course, they let their fighting stance go, because I'm giving them some recognition. That's what they really wanted."

CHAPTER 11
The Definitive Book on Speaking

Speak and Grow Rich

"When you write a book, as you know because you are an author," Dottie told me, "people will come up to you with the book you wrote. It's tattered and worn out. They'll say, 'I'm embarrassed to ask you to autograph it, but I just got so much good out of it.' I always take their hand and say, 'That's the nicest thing you could tell me! Because you know who you are?' And they'll say, 'Well, I think so.' I'll say, 'I know who you are. You're the one I wrote it for! You're the one!" Dottie wrote her books for thousands of such "ones."

In 1989, Dottie and her daughter Lilly, wrote the book that is still used as the bible for professional speakers, "Speak and Grow Rich." Who better to write this book than the leading lady of speaking? Earl Nightingale wrote the foreword. Here is an excerpt:

"Dottie Walters just doesn't quit. She has never quit. She doesn't slow down, and I hope to God she never does. We need her. In addition to being a world-class expert at what she does, Dottie Walters is a kind, loving, helpful person who has never for a moment lost her human touch. By all means read 'Speak and Grow Rich.' You'll get to meet these remarkable women. They are in every paragraph, and the love comes shining through, clear, and bright. I cannot recommend this book too highly. I hope it sells a million copies every year."

Earl Nightingale also said, "She has that special talent of putting her thoughts into words so that the words go out and move people."

Today people like Jack Canfield write of *Speak and Grow Rich*: "I love this book! I love the authors, Dottie and Lily Walters. We are proud to feature their stories in our *Chicken Soup for the Soul* books." And as an aside, Jack Canfield and Mark Victor Hansen were with Dottie discussing the success of their first *Chicken Soup* book. They wondered what to call the sequel. Dottie said that since it was soup, why not call it *A 2nd Helping?* The idea lady did it again!

And perhaps one of the highest compliments came from British humorist, Graham Davis, who said of her book, "The value of the information inside cannot be calculated. I hope that none of my rivals in the UK *ever* gets to see a copy!"

The core of Dottie's advice is timeless. That is apparent to those who know her or who have read her advice. She knows her game in the selling and speaking arena.

Nan Pratt said, "Dottie will be up there speaking and tell you how to do this or that. She'll tell you in a most graceful way how not to do something. Once Dottie walked close to the stage when a group of women were talking loud and said, 'I'm sure you have something very interesting to say and I'd love to hear it after I'm through speaking.' When Dottie gets up to speak, you know immediately she knows what she's talking about and that she's a great marketer. She's done her homework. So many people have said, 'She's helped me more than any one."

There was no one better to write that book on speaking and promotion of speaking careers than Dottie Walters and her daughter Lilly. Dottie recently said of the speaking world. "I've been in it for so many years. It's like home."

CHAPTER 12
The Same Ideas for Success

*"It's the biggest, most important people
who take time to remember the little things."*
Dottie Walters

The Napoleon Hill Foundation

A non-profit educational institution dedicated to making
the world a better place in which to live.

Box 1721

Columbia, South Carolina

Altamont Road No.5
Greenville, S. C.
November 23, 1962.

My dear Dorothy Walters:

Congratulations! You've made the Big Leap
of authoring, and may I thank you warmly for the auto
of your book which you sent to my Chicago office, and
that I consider it a masterpiece?

Today Mrs. Hill and I were watching Telet
The Truth" came on. Of course, I recognized you as I h

**A portion of the letter Napoleon Hill sent to
congratulate Dottie.**

Napoleon Hill and Dr. Peale

Napoleon Hill was very inspiring to Dottie. And so was her
great mentor, Dr. Peale. She wants to tell everyone, "If you
haven't read his books, go to the library and find him. Tell him I
said, 'Hello!' I've read all of his books and I sure recommend

them to you. His *Power of Positive Thinking* would always give me a great lift. It's just wonderful!" I can attest to this. She keeps both Hill's and Peale's books handy on her shelf and has more than once pointed out to me the color of Peale's book – bright red.

Dottie gleaned much from the authors and speakers she has met or read about. She said, "One of the things that hit me right away was that these people of accomplishment had the same ideas." She felt that these great minds should have sat down at a table together to share ideas. She said they actually did have a television show called, "The Meeting of the Minds." This was Steve Allen's award-wining program from the 1970's where people dressed up as the icons from different generations and discuss ideas. "Perhaps," she said. "Ben Franklin would be talking to one of the great Caesars from Rome. They were from different generations and from different years, but they had wonderful discussion groups." She wishes that they would bring that type of TV show back.

Bruce Barton

Another author and speaker who influenced Dottie was Bruce Barton. "Oh my goodness!" she said. "He was a brilliant man, just a brilliant man! After I got to know him, he encouraged me and wrote to me several times. When you have somebody of great repute who is taking the time to give you a hand of some kind, you have to do it! You just have to rise to it!" Dottie said that because Barton was such a popular man, she almost felt she didn't deserve for him to be interested in her. But Bruce Barton was known as a very kind man who always encouraged everybody around him, including Dottie.

The goal is that we all have access to great minds around us, but we also have access to our own great mind. We are the ones that have to use it in order for it to work for us. "That is why God gave it to you," Dottie said smiling.

Her Mentors

Dottie read books, on or written by, as many inspiring people as she could. "The great ideas of the world have been called The Great Conversation – a stream of ideas that are available to everyone," she said. A book that surprised her because she didn't think she could comprehend it, was Einstein's. Dottie said. "My favorite quote by Einstein was when he said, 'Remember, the solution is always located at hand.' At hand! Now how close is your hand? It's here! You're missing it. Start looking around better, because whatever you need, could be right here close to you, but you are not reaching for it. Then all you have to do is start reaching! Solutions are at hand." She wants to get that into everyone's mind. Dottie said "When we have challenges, if we'd just stop and be quiet and think, *THE SOLUTION IS AT HAND.* Then just let that thought run around in your head. There it is!" It was true for her. "The solution always was there... waiting for me!" she said.

How did she get her solutions? She got quiet and listened for them. Dottie wants you to know that there is always a solution. She is living proof of that, because she's always found one, or sometimes several solutions, because she got still and expected a solution to appear.

I was curious how Dottie paid attention to her "Friends of the Mind" so she could hear their advice and wisdom. "By reading," she said. "Then I hear their voices. I'm really truly not a nut. But I can hear that mental voice."

Dottie told me something interesting about great people. "I found that the more important the person was that I was working with, like Napoleon Hill, the nicer he was to me," she said. Most people think it is just the opposite. She became acquainted with a number of great minds like Barton, and Hill. One of them once told her "I couldn't believe that you were a woman!" because of her ability to think like the successful men did.

Good Leaders

"All great leaders emerge when a crisis occurs."
Dottie Walters

Dottie is a great leader herself. She has guided hundreds of future leaders on their way to their leadership roles. When I asked Dottie about the qualities of good leaders, she again told a story that demonstrates the qualities that she holds in high esteem.

"Good leaders always understand that they have to find the secret gift in every man or woman who is on their team," said Dottie. She said Caesar used to go down by the campfires of his troops at night, because they were fighting the next morning. Caesar would put his hand on each soldier's shoulder and say, "I remember that you are so good at (whatever task the man excelled at). We are counting on you!" Dottie said, "Caesar would go around to the next little fire and the next. As he walked away from each little group, they would call after him in Latin, 'There goes the boss, he's never discouraged!' That's one of the great characteristics of a leader in anything. You don't go around saying, 'This won't work,' and all that bad stuff. You say, 'Follow me' and 'We need you. Your talents are important to us."

Another story she told me was one she felt demonstrated great leadership. The sequel to the book *Mutiny on the Bounty,* is called, *Men Against the Sea.* Dottie found it to be a fascinating book. "If you haven't read it, you are in for a treat," she said. The essence of the story was that Captain Bligh was cast out to the ocean in an open boat with the men who had worked for him on the *Bounty,* along with a few extra men who had been in jail. Bligh sat at the back of the boat steering. Under the seat were all of the navigation maps of how to go by the stars.

I'll let Dottie tell the rest of the story in her own special way. "The first thing Bligh did was to ask each man if he would accept him as his leader. Bligh said, 'I need you because you are so good at (whatever that man excelled at).' He did exactly what Caesar had done in Rome. Perhaps one man was good at putting out a fishing line so they had food to eat. Each man said, 'Yes, I accept you as my leader.' He wasn't the terrible man who was portrayed in the first book. This was what he was really like. When they finally got to port early one morning, Bligh was still tied to the tiller. He'd never moved that whole time! The others were all passed out, sick, or asleep in the boat. But Bligh steered the boat in by the sails. They sailed up to the dock at daybreak. The sun was just coming up and a little boy ran out to them. Captain Bligh said to the boy, 'Go get your boss and have him come here.' That little boy said, 'Aye, aye,' and did as he was told. When the boss came back, only then did Bligh take the chains off, stand up and say, 'Permission to come aboard, sir.' I thought 'He did it right. He did it right!' He honored the other man by letting him be the boss. It was his island so it was the proper thing to do - to request permission to come aboard." Dottie felt that gesture showed respect and that a great leader always shows respect for others.

Dottie was impressed that Bligh's leadership had resulted in the loss of only one man on that whole trip. He brought the rest of his men through. "That's my definition of a leader," Dottie said. Dottie has brought many people through the seas of success. Even though she wrote to help women, she has helped make many men very successful too.

> *"When we become master of ourselves, it will then follow*
> *that we can become leaders of others."*
> Dottie Walters

Dottie never takes the credit for someone's success. "You had it in you in the first place. I just switched on the light," Dottie tells her clients. "I remind them that I didn't create them, God did.

That's far more accurate and empowering to them. Then they know it was inside them all along," she said. "We all need that confidence."

"When someone gets a setback and they think, 'God doesn't want me to do this,' you must tell yourself, 'No. That's not true. I'll do it and I'll do it wonderfully,' she said. "God believed you could do it, but *you* have to make up your mind to do it."

CHAPTER 13
At the Ranch

Dottie at her "Scottish Castle"

When I stayed at her ranch overnight, Dottie always delighted in watching the birds in the mornings. The little creatures would fly right up to her dining room window in swooping feathery clouds and perch on her bird feeder. She'd tell me to watch because the little birds would throw most of the seed on the ground and then take some back to the Oleander bushes for their babies. She mentioned once that she wished she had a book on birds so she could tell what kind of birds they were. I found a bird book, wrote a poem in it and sent the book to her. She always keeps that book handy on her dining room table. Little things like that mean a great deal to her. Gestures of friendship and kindness, which she herself has always shown to people.

One of the first things she showed me at her ranch was the avocado tree. Many people in Southern California have avocado trees, but Dottie's avocado tree comes with a bear. Yes, a real bear! He climbs up the tree and throws down the avocados. The first night I stayed at the ranch, I jumped at every little noise because that tree was just outside the lovely pink guest room Dottie fixed up for me for the night. No, I never did see the bear, but there was often evidence he (or she?) was there. I wrote a poem about Dottie's bear. It's at the end of the book.

Not only does Dottie share her brilliant ideas, but she shares whatever she loves. She gave me beautiful geraniums from her garden. When I tell her how lovely they are growing, she says, "Be sure to tell them 'Hello' from me." I am sure they appreciate her well wishes.

Starting the Day with Dottie

Sometimes when I stayed at the ranch, Dottie's good friend Jim, who lives on the ranch, joined us for our morning coffee chats. What fun discussing the many ideas that sprung up being around Dottie. She seems to grow ideas! Dottie is a very creative soul. Ideas flow freely from her. "There's no limit to ideas!" she says. Everyone should wake up and have coffee or a morning drink with someone as charming and insightful as Dottie.

Messages of Inspiration

To be sure there have been difficulties and setbacks along the way. Generally each one of them has helped me to grow."
Dottie Walters

Dottie has a sign up in her office, "Who needs what I've got?" She says, "If you keep thinking that way, that's your market. That's who will buy it from you. Whether you have a speech, a book, or an audio, it gets to be where your mind starts working like that right away." I think that this simple advice is perhaps some of her most brilliant. Every successful person must find a way to create value. She just gave you the key.

"One of the places you can find a lot of ideas like that, is in your mailbox," says Dottie. "I want all of you to stop saying that it's junk mail. It's not. It's opportunity mail!"

So how do you look for opportunities in their mail? Here is Dottie's answer. "You find somebody who is advertising and has something they want to sell. You think, 'Could they use what I've got? Do they need what I've got?' Then you call them on the phone. That's how I sold that album. It was the chapter that the book people didn't want, so I sold it to the audio people!"

Everything was usable to Dottie. Everything had value. By thinking that way, she continually brought more value into the world. She actually created it. Otherwise we would not have had the wisdom contained in *The Seven Secrets of Selling to Women*, or the immense help to speakers around the world with *Speak and Grow Rich*.

CHAPTER 14
The Gift Within

"If you use the gifts that God gives you,
you can do what God wants you to."
Dottie Walters

Dottie always warm and gracious,
welcomed the opportunities of life.

D ottie's grandfather believed in her. Dottie felt that some of us were lucky enough to have a schoolteacher, a relative, or perhaps a neighbor that believed we had talent and encouraged us. Abraham Lincoln did. Abe's father remarried after his wife died. His new stepmother was very kind to Abe and taught him to read. And of course we know the story about Abe walking miles through the snow and all night to borrow a book and bring it back when he promised. Dottie admired any lover of books but especially liked the way Abe honored his stepmother. Dottie felt that he respected her and admired her. He never got too "important" to show that respect and concern for others. When Abe was elected president he said, "Everything I am and can do, I owe to my angel mother." Dottie said, "When I read that about him, I thought, 'What a nice man to acknowledge his mom! Even though she wasn't his birth mother, she was loving to him.'" Dottie thought that took a lot of guts on his stepmother's part. "She must have been a great mother," Dottie said, "especially since that was not her own son. You usually are more forgiving to your own children."

Believe in Your Gifts and Use Them

*"The only handle that guarantees success
is on your side of the door."*
Dottie Walters

It's a great gift when we can have other people who believe in us, especially when we are small, but we need that encouragement at any age. It is also really important that we believe in ourselves and our own gifts because we all have them. Dottie absolutely believes this about everyone, including you.

Dottie instills in you the desire to live up to her great expectations of you. She remarked, "Everyone of you reading this, has gifts to develop. Quit saying 'I can't,' or 'It won't work.' Think of how it *will* work. Think who needs that gift of yours?" She clearly sees the gifts wrapped within each person. It is her amazing talent to get people to open and share their own gifts. "That is between you and your heavenly Father," Dottie said. "If he didn't want you to have the gifts he gave you, then why would he have given them to you? They are yours. I always think God must feel bad when you don't use them."

She once told me, "You can write poetry, which is a great gift and you can play the piano, which is another great gift. God surely wants you to use the gifts that He gave you." When I get busy, it's easy to push the things that come naturally and easily to me, like music and poetry, into the background, and focus instead on the things I have to struggle to do. But remembering Dottie's advice has helped me tremendously to not neglect my natural talents and share those gifts with the world.

Your Own Talents

Dottie knows that everyone has the internal power for success. "What work leaves you with a glowing sense of accomplishment? Here lies a talent and no matter how small it is now it can grow." Dottie nailed the secret to success. "Be sure you build soaring castles in the air! But be doubly sure you have also built a strong foundation under them. Your vision comes first in the form of your castles in the air. With your vision firmly in mind, set yourself a goal - which is your foundation - and step by step - climb up."

Locating Talents

Dottie told me she recently got a letter from someone who was a little discouraged. The young man told Dottie, "I don't have any gifts, so there is no use in me trying to do anything. I'll never amount to anything." That was the wrong person to tell those words to!

She wrote back and said, "Don't you ever say that again. I want you to realize that the moment you were conceived, God your heavenly Father, gave you great gifts. Are you going to thank him by never using them? Never opening them? If you were a father how would you feel about your child who would do that?" The young man said that he hadn't thought of it that way. Dottie told him he should think about it, which I'm sure he did after hearing her response! She also gave him several of her favorite quotes to help him.

Depreciation

*"Within each of us is a reservoir of inspiration and intuition –
the source of all good and creative emotions, the source of all
constructive, positive, driving force.
Draw upon this Higher Power."*
Dottie Walters

"I believe that sometimes people think that being humble is a great virtue," Dottie says. "It could be if you were a braggart or something like that. But don't depreciate yourself - that means to lower in value. Realize that every gift that you have been given is a heavenly gift. Why would God give it if he didn't want you to use it? I want you to use it. God wants you to use it. And as far as being humble, help everybody around you! When you give the gift of helping others, you're going to find it repaid a thousand fold."

Dottie's grandson, Michael, whose last name is MacFarlane from their Scottish clan, is the president of the MacFarlane clan - all of them in the world. He was planning a trip to Scotland and invited all the clan members to go on the trip to see the places where their ancestors came from. Loch Lomond in Scotland is the clan's homeland. Michael wrote in the headline of a flyer he sent to the clan, "Your Ancestors Are Calling You!" Dottie loved that headline and translated Michael's message to everyone, "Your talents are calling you. Your talents are calling! So use them! Just remember that you have to work at it."

Find a Way to Be Useful

*"Remember that you only pass this way once in your lifetime,
so try to lift people up whenever and wherever you can."*
Dottie Walters

"Nothing great was ever accomplished without somebody working at it, thinking of new ways," she said. She refers again to Franklin's many inventions because he spent time thinking about creating things that everybody needed. Before the Franklin stove, everyone's house got full of smoke and soot. Franklin decided it would be better to send it out of the house not into the house. Sounds pretty logical to me but no one had done it before. Then he sent up the famous kite that led to the invention of the lightening rod. Dottie said. "He was always thinking of something else. Then he wouldn't just let it stay as a thought, he'd make it into a physical thing. Many of them did very well." Dottie was a huge fan of Franklin's creative thought process.

"Franklin thought about what kind of a book he could publish that would be of great help to the most Americans," she said. "He thought what they really needed to know about was about the weather. So he got it all figured out. I don't quite know how he did it, but he did it. He wrote almanacs. The almanacs told farmers when to plant their seeds and when to harvest them. They had to keep the almanacs coming out because the times for planting changed every year. He let each of the young men that he set up in business, sell the almanacs. Franklin made a fortune with that. It saved all the crops because they knew when to plant them."

In the world of today and the challenges we face, if every one of us would just look around and think, and be open to ideas, look at what we could do!

"Do you remember there was a scene in the movie *Braveheart,* where the British had gotten the Irish to fight on their side?" Dottie asked. "They were fighting the Scots and started towards each other. Suddenly they get close enough to start identifying each other. The Irish yell, 'Ah look, there's my cousin! How's the wife?' He yells back, 'She's fine! She's going to have another baby!' They all put their arms down and wouldn't fight each other! I love that scene from *Braveheart!* That's how we all should be. Quit fighting and do something useful!"

Ask Don't Complain

Dottie has great advice about not being negative. She says, "Instead of saying, 'I can't do this. I can't do that.' Say, 'Yes I can.' When you go to sleep at night, put it on your mind and say, 'Father, I need an idea for an invention, I need an idea for a book, an idea for a speech, whatever it is that you want to do, please help me.' Then go to sleep. In the morning you wake up and say, 'Ah, there it is!'"

Renewal

Dottie refers to a quote by Shakespeare. "The sun will not be up as soon as I to greet the fair adventure of tomorrow." Dottie said Shakespeare was referring to the renewal that sleep gives us in every way, both physical and mental. She feels that when you wake up, it's a very good time to sit down and start writing your book, or figure out a new topic for your speech. The next question to ask yourself is, "Who needs this?" That's what Franklin did. He thought of who needed the almanacs. It was the farmers. They counted on it. She felt that's why America got going, because farmers would know when to plant the crops. And that's because Ben had done some very good thinking to help them.

Unseen Help

One thing I believe is that there are people who have gone on before us, people in heaven or the afterlife, who are up there cheering for us, wanting us to succeed. I asked Dottie if she felt that way too, that there is an unseen world, cheering for us to do our best. Here is her reply. "Oh yes. I felt that God was helping me in every way. If I would do my part, then I wasn't going to lose that house. We were not going to lose it."

If anyone of you reading this is in a struggle right now, look at what Dottie has done with her life. She has told me many times, "If I could do it, and look at what I started with, then you can do it too." She has deep faith in your ability to live a successful life, one where you can contribute your part. The rest of the world needs that gift of yours.

CHAPTER 15
The Poetic Lady

Dottie has written poetry from the time she was a little girl. Her first poem was published at eight years old. It's one of the things that instantly connected us as friends. We love each other's poetry for we both love words and uplifting thoughts. Dottie said that when she writes poetry she always hears a little melody with it. She asked me if that happens when I write poetry. She was very interested in how the creative process works in different people.

"It comes dancing into my head and I have to grab a piece of paper and write it down," said Dottie. 'It always feel like it's kind of musical. I know that you are very musical playing the piano," she told me, "and that you write a lot of poetry too, so we have that in common. It's another form of communication with people, and I get a lot of joy out of it." She just loves poetry.

The Stolen Poem

Not all of Dottie's experiences with poetry were positive. The following story illustrates that, but it also contains such an important point. The first time Dottie went to an NSA meeting, (National Speakers Association) she gave out copies of a poem she had written, including a copy to a particular man. In place of a business card, she had made her poem her calling card by putting her name, address and phone number across the bottom, along with a byline on it. At the next meeting she attended, that man was passing out sheets of paper at the event. Dottie asked him, "Oh, I see you used my idea and are doing the same thing!" He handed Dottie one of them. It was a little too much of the same thing! "It was my poem!" said Dottie. "He stole it! She asked him why he didn't think of his own poem. She told him he probably could have thought of something much better. The man replied, "I know you didn't write this!" Dottie asked why he thought that. He told Dottie, "Well, you're not bright enough!" She thought to herself, "Oh, you poor man. You don't have love for other people and you can't believe in them. I am sorry for you."

When people have said things like that to Dottie, she has able been able to rethink it and tell herself, "No, there's another way. A positive and a better way." She says that you have to believe that in your own heart. She told me that man never wrote a book or did anything in the speaking world. "He dropped out of speaking not long after that, so he was no competitor to me anyway," she said. "But I would have helped him if he had asked me."

There was an opportunity right at his hand. But more impressive was Dottie's thinking. She still would have helped the man to succeed... if he had but asked.

CHAPTER 16
The Loch Sloy Hero

**The letter Dottie's beloved grandfather brought
with him to the United States.**

"I have to say my first hero was my grandfather, who was Scottish," Dottie said. "It was he who gave me the best advice. He sang me the song *Scotland the Brave*. If you have ever heard or seen a Scottish bagpipe band come marching down the street playing *Scotland the Brave*, oh, my gosh! I just about float up in the air because it just moves me so! I think of that wonderful man, my grandpa!"

Dottie's grandfather and two of his younger brothers were orphans when they came to America alone. They went to Chicago because that was where the action was going on with all the machinery being built back then in the industrial age.

Her grandfather, Robert, was an inventor. He found out that the trains had to stop every so many miles. The train workers had to get out with water and a hose. Then they'd walk along the train and water down the hot wheels so they wouldn't catch on fire. Robert saw an opportunity here. He invented something to put on the wheels of the trains of that period to keep them from catching fire. "If the wheels caught on fire, they would make everyone get off the train. You can just imagine that," Dottie said. That made a huge difference. The trains were now able to go across the country faster.

"My grandfather got a job with a company that made windmills," Dottie said. "The company told him that they would teach him to be an engineer if he'd come and work for them. He said that he'd be proud to do that. I can remember him talking about that. I'd say, 'Grandpa, what's an engineer?' Her grandfather said, 'The engineer is the one who 'drives the dream."

"One time we were in their house in Chicago which he'd bought from the royalties from one of his patents," Dottie said. "Everyone else had gone shopping. They left me home with Grandpa. We were sitting on the big screened-in porch that looked out on the alley. The little girl from the lower flat and I were playing with our dolls. I tried to stand up and slipped on something and tore my leg. It was bleeding. So of course I yelled like most kids would. I saw grandpa and ran up the stairs. He said, 'Lassie, what is it?' I said, 'I'm bleeding and I've been hurt.' He said, 'You come over here. I want you to remember. We Scots never give up. We never give up!' Then he said, 'Now, you sit here on my lap,' and he lifted me up. He put his arm around me very tenderly and said, 'I want you to look at your left hand, palm up. Take your right hand with your fingers around just below your wrist so that your four fingers are right below your thumb, and very gently press.' I asked him, 'What is that?' I was too little to know anything about pulses. He said, 'Those are the Scottish drums and they are always with you! We Scots may get knocked down, but we never stay down. Never! We *never* stay down.' He said, 'Now listen again. What else do you hear?' I said, 'I don't know, Grandpa, I still feel the drums.' 'Listen, listen!' he said, 'That's the bagpipes coming! Can you hear them?' Then he sang me the song, *Scotland the Brave*. I can still see it and feel it in my heart and visualize it again. He was a great man."

Runways of Success

"After all, I told myself when I got discouraged;
I can't afford not to learn."
Dottie Walters

Dottie was influenced by a significant number of incredible men but there were also some women, especially one in particular who made a huge difference to Dottie when she was about to graduate from high school.

"I was working early one morning on some things. Bob was still overseas at this time. I had been reading Amelia Earhart's biography. My three friends from high school called me. One told me, 'I've been accepted to this college,' and one said, 'I've been accepted to this university, and I'm going to go.' It just hit me that I wasn't going to get to go to college. I guess I thought that my journalism teacher would tell me about some journalist scholarship somewhere, but she never mentioned it. I felt left behind. I was sitting there and I had this book of hers in front of me. This is what she said:

'Some of us have great runways already built for us,
If you've got a runway, take off!

But if you haven't, then understand
It is your own responsibility to grab a shovel
And to build a runway for yourself
And all those who will surely follow you!'

Thank goodness Dottie didn't get to college. Greater things were waiting in the wings for her. Dottie may have missed her opportunity of a lifetime had she been sitting in a classroom instead of her own home. She took Amelia Earhart's advice and has built runways in many areas in life for both herself and for others to take off on. One of her greatest joys is when she can help someone to "fly." "I am so thrilled when somebody tells me that they were able to use the idea I gave them and it worked!" she says.

"If you needed courage and if I helped you to find it,
then I'd be honored."
Dottie Walters

CHAPTER 17
The Dragon of Opportunity

Dottie holding one of her precious dragons.

"Hidden in trouble lies the key, our own magnificent opportunity."
Dottie Walters

*"Remember the door to opportunity has only one knob - on the inside.
No one else can open that door for you."*
Dottie Walters

Dottie loves dragons. She has a huge collection of them. One of the first things she told me about when I went to her ranch was the dragon and what it symbolizes. It goes with her whole philosophy of life. It symbolizes opportunity.

Dottie believes that she first read about the dragon in the *Reader's Digest*. The Chinese people believe the dragon's real name is "enterprise." "To be enterprising is to work, to do something, to create something," she said. "The dragon always has a pearl in his hand. Look at the next Chinese dragon that you see. Sometimes it looks like a round ball, depending on where it comes from. Sometimes it's an actual pearl that you will see in his hand. The name of the pearl is "potentiality." *Enterprise* and *Potentiality*. With those two together, there is no stopping you! The dragon is throwing pearls at us all the time. Some people never catch them, because they say, 'Oh well, surely he doesn't mean me. I'm not good enough to do it,' something negative like that. So quit saying that! Stop that!"

Dottie is a firm believer in talking positively to yourself - and that lends itself to talking positively to others. She knows that what you tell yourself is what matters, not what anyone else tells you.

"Because you and God can make it," she says. "God is on your side! Why else would he give you a talent for writing, speaking, or painting houses? I don't care whatever it is." Those of you reading this, you're reading Dottie's messages for a reason right now! And Dottie will never forget to tell you the most important message that was ever given to her, "Never give up. Never give up!" Whenever she mentioned this to me, she always said it at least twice. She said, "Look at all the things in this world that we wouldn't have, like airplanes and computers, if someone didn't find a way to do it."

"There's not an opportunity that she's missed," says Dottie's friend Nan Pratt. "Dottie takes every opportunity that comes by. She can sniff them out."

"When opportunity comes, grab it!"
Dottie Walters

Dottie has helped me with countless opportunities. She talked to me about Irwin Zucker and the Book Publicists of Southern California meetings in such a way that I thought she must miss those meetings. I asked her if she would like to attend a meeting. I think she truly appreciated that, so I talked to our friend Jack Nichols about going to a meeting. Jack met us at Dottie's and drove. Those were such special times for all of us. I know it was because of Dottie's influence that my first book won a 2005 "Irwin Award" in the humanitarian category She was with me when I received it and so very happy for me. She had just helped someone succeed and that was her greatest pleasure.

CHAPTER 18
The Biggest Lesson

"If you make up your mind to do something, there's always a way."
Dottie Walters

Dottie Saw the Extraordinary in the Ordinary

The biggest question I asked Dottie was, "What have you learned most from life?" She said, "That hope is located at hand. Don't despair, because it is very close to you." Dottie said, "When my husband died, I thought that I couldn't stand that for a while. But he has always been close to me since. He's right close at hand. He used to call me 'Momma,' and it made me so mad, because I used to say, 'I'm your sweetheart, not your mother! Quit calling me *Momma!*"

"One day he told me, 'I want you to know why I call you *Momma.*' I said, 'Well, I'd really like to know why you do that.'

Bob said, 'Because you are the mother of my children and that's the dearest gift that you could ever give me.' I said, 'Oh, I apologize, I'm sorry! I didn't know that's what you meant."

"One night not long after he died, I heard him calling me, calling *Momma. Momma! Momma!"* I woke up and said, 'Is it you?' Bob said, 'Yes.' Our grandson's wife was expecting. We didn't know the sex of the baby. Bob could put his hand on a woman and tell her the sex of the baby. He never failed. He was always right. I thought maybe he'd seen the baby, because it wasn't born yet. Bob said, 'I want you to know that it's a girl.' And it was a girl when she born! They gave her the name *Kaylee,* which in the Scottish dialect means, "celebrate." Her last name is King, so she is Kaylee King. It sounds musical, doesn't it?" she said delighted.

I asked Dottie if she thought people are predestined to meet and if she thought she was destined to meet Bob. "Yes," Dottie said. She told me a little story about their first meeting. "My mother was taking me to a place for ballroom dancing. We would go on Friday evenings and learn a new step. Then there was open dancing where they encouraged us to dance and try out some of the things they taught us. Bob walked up to me and invited me to dance. That's how I met him."

"I had to laugh because I was only fifteen," she said. "I'd never had a date with a boy in my life! The teacher was kind of mad because Bob had come over and asked me to dance. She told Bob, 'You know that that girl is *fast.'* Fast? I had never even had a date! Bob said that encouraged him a lot! Of course Bob was kidding her. He came back after the dance and asked Dottie for a date. They were inseparable after that. Only a world war took them apart. But their hearts never have left each other.

I asked Dottie what she learned from her husband? "I think to be very loving," she said. "He never got mad at anybody. He was good to everyone that knew him. Everybody loved him." Dottie talked with pride that Bob was named after Robert Emmet, an

Irish orator and patriot, who was killed by the English in the early 1800s. She had enormous respect for her husband.

Dottie and Bob, her cowboy.

Dottie had some beautiful men in her life and she had some that gave her some challenges. But she had a lot more beautiful help. "Oh my goodness, how grateful I am! So grateful," she said.

A Classy Lady

"Remember that you can't say 'Thank you,' too many times."
Dottie Walters

Almost everyone I have talked to about Dottie feels the same way. She has class. Joe Kessler said, "Dottie multi-tasked. I don't know how she did it. She was a speaker, ran a magazine, a bureau, put out books, had a family. She was high energy and very warm and receptive. I've never met anybody who traveled so extensively. Dottie is an unbelievable woman. I have a tremendous amount of respect for her. She is first a terrific writer and a great listener. She knows how to speak in front of any group. Today, she probably would've been in the White House."

Elegant wherever she appeared, that was Dottie.

Friend, Nan Pratt said, "She just loves people. She's always so happy. Dottie has character and integrity; especially intellectual integrity and can remain focused even when things aren't 100%. She encourages others through their own disappointments and challenges. I admire her ability to remain strong. Dottie focuses on others rather than herself. She always had that ability to move forward. I've never heard her to be sarcastic. She can be witty and funny however."

I can attest to this. In June of 2006, Dottie spoke to the Speakers Bureau of Orange County, California. Dottie described her conversation with a large bookseller. She had found out that some bookstores let people eat food and sweets while they read the new books. Dottie thought about this and foresaw potential problems for the authors. She asked what the stores did with all those 'dirty books." As she realized what she was saying, she quickly clarified. "Well, I don't mean dirty books, as in x-rated," she charmingly smiled. The audience howled at the thought of this sweet, woman talking about dirty books. "A good laugh is always great," Dottie told me. "but be careful not to step on anyone's toes or hurt anyone."

Lori Akina of NSA, Greater LA says of Dottie, "She is top notch, just cream of the crop. She always has the great appearance. It's wonderful, just to see her in the room. She is a very classy lady." Elmer Wheeler, a prominent speaker said he was "convinced Dottie is the best 'salesman in skirts he has ever heard of. And the smartest sizzling salesman there is around."

There is no doubt that Dottie Walters is no ordinary woman. There is no doubt that she has helped countless people become successful and develop their gifts. She came into the world with a glorious character and lived her life brilliantly. We are all the better for the gift of a Scottish woman who never gave up.

Her entire life is about service.

Dottie Parting Advice

"I'd like to say to all of you that if you could think about what my grandfather told me. If you feel like things aren't going well, put your finger around your wrist. Feel that beat. You know that it's there. It's hope. It's inspiration. It's everything that God intended the moment that you were conceived, because he gave you a whole lot of gifts. You haven't begun to use them all! Remember that and put your fingers below your thumb and see what you feel."

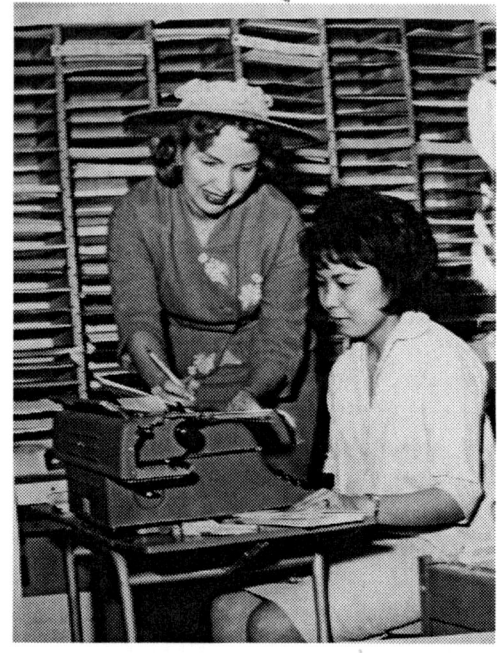

"The greatest gift you can give to anyone is your attention."
Dottie Walters

Much success to you in looking for and finding all those opportunities that are out there, right now, just waiting for you, close at hand.

PART II
Dottie's Life Lessons

14 LESSONS THAT CAN CHANGE YOUR LIFE

"When I started all I had was a basket."

Dottie Walters

WHY I WROTE DOTTIE'S LIFE LESSONS

Dottie and I often had coffee in the morning together when I stayed overnight at the ranch. We'd talk about everything, but Dottie would always have ideas, suggestions and fantastic stories. From those coffee talks and our drives to Hollywood with our friend, Jack Nichols, came a suggestion that we do a CD project together. We had a great time planning the project, doing the interviews and working on the book. Looking through Dottie's photo albums was a treat as she explained who the letters were from, and expanded on the stories she told me. Dottie loves people. She loves inspiring ideas. She loves her Scottish ancestry.

We did the interview in her den where she has her famous soda fountain. It is decorated with her many "dragons of opportunity" given to her by people all over the world.

After we did the interview about her life story, I decided to write Life Lessons from Dottie like I do with my Hero column, *Heroes Among Us*. It was Dottie who guided me through the process of doing the column, negotiating the rights, getting the Wal-Mart sponsorship and writing my books. We both love poetry and Dottie would often give me her charming poems as a gift right before I left her ranch. One day she asked me if I thought I could write some music to her poems because when she writes them, she hears music with them. I said, I didn't know if I could, but I would try. The result is a CD to her poem called, "Loch Sloy."

I benefited enormously from Dottie's gifts as have many others. They are too good to keep in one person. They are meant to be shared.

Here are those lessons for you, from a lady who always looks for opportunities in life.

Terri Marie

The Solution is at Hand, The Dottie Walters Story   105

DOTTIE'S LIFE LESSONS AND HOW YOU CAN APPLY THEM IN YOUR OWN LIFE

From the Solution is at Hand, The Dottie Walters Story are great lessons that Dottie has learned in her life. Around a light as bright as Dottie's is, you grow a little brighter too. You see things that you might not have seen before. Dottie illuminates the pathway to success for you. You see it more clearly. She has the gift of vision and understanding. Here are some life lessons from the Dottie Walters Story.

#1 God is on Your Side

Dottie feels that God is here to help you, not to punish you. God gives each of us gifts, but he expects us to use those gifts. To paraphrase Mike Dooley, "You go one inch, the universe will go a foot, but you go first." You choose to do things differently when you know God is on your side. You take more risks. You choose things you love, knowing that God put those things in your heart for a good reason. What would you do if you knew God would help you? A lot more, Dottie and I are sure of it. God gives you not just the dream, but the "scheme" to accomplish it. The help may be an urge to stop by a particular place or to call someone. You may see a message on a billboard, or card, or magazine, that has your answer or your next step clearly spelled out for you. But one thing is certain - it's close by.

Remember Dottie's advice that she gleaned from Einstein, "The Solution is at Hand." Imprint that on your brain so that you know it down to your bones.

Dottie says, "I personally believe that God gave every one of us wonderful gifts the moment of conception. So when we use the gift, whatever it is, do it. Do it with a will and a passion so that God is proud of you."

Everybody has that ability. Every one of us. God didn't forget a single human. Each was given a gift. Find it.

Dottie said, "Just like we all have the ability to breathe, and to eat, and to walk. God used a good pattern." He is ALWAYS on YOUR side.

#2 Admire Great Minds

It started with Ben Franklin, then Einstein, Amelia Earhart, and hundreds of others. They are the great minds that Dottie has connected with, many of them through their books in the library. The library or the bookstore is there for all of us to benefit from.

Dottie knew that you meet great people at the library. We have equal rights to those words of knowledge. Words with wisdom in them are timeless.

The following quote by Ben Franklin will apply to our great, great, grandchildren as much as it applies to us.

"If a man empties his purse into his head, no man can take it away from him. An investment in knowledge always pays the best interest!"

Dottie admired Ben and wrote a charming poem about Ben Franklin's accomplishments.

"This is a poem that I wrote about Benjamin Franklin, who I am very fond of, and I think he is fond of me too," said Dottie.

Ben Franklin: My Love!
They laughed and derided.
"Go fly a kit. Ben!"
But Ben just kept smiling.
A wise man, Ye Ken?
He reached to the lightning
And tamed that wild beast.
He charted the oceans!
Ben's thoughts are like yeast,
Wherever he traveled
Minds Western or East.

Inquiring and learning
Exchanging a feast…
Of new ways to do things
With freedom and song!
I long for this friendship
I yearn to belong,
To Ben's merry company,
When my life is frightful,
Then I read his stories
His spirit delightful!
He sends hopes like kites up
"With teamwork, we CAN!
There's naught who can stop us…
COME, HERE IS A PLAN!
Ben opens the floodgates
Of Genius for me,
Inventor, and statesman
With bright strategy.
His favorite expression
Of all I have read
"NOW, LET'S DO THE BUSINESS!
Come! Just use your head!"
Adored by the ladies
They loved him! Their "Sun!"
Now, need I inform you,
This lady is one?

Ben Franklin is one of Dottie's great loves. But there were many other men throughout time that she greatly admired. Shakespeare for instance. She often quoted him in our conversations.

Shakespearean Delight

Dottie deeply admired Shakespeare, She said, "Shakespeare had wonderful, wonderful things that he said. I think one of my favorite quotes is when he has Romeo say to Juliet when she comes out on her balcony, "She hangs upon the cheek of night, like a pearl in an Ethiope's ear." And of course, right away you can think about the dark night and her being lighted up. That's how he saw her."

One thing Dottie loved was Shakespeare's special gift of getting right to the essence of something. She related his plays to learning how to speak. That is the core of professional speaking of which Shakespeare is a master. Who better to teach how to inspire audiences than Shakespeare?

"Shakespeare is wonderful," said Dottie. "Many, many of his lines are terrific. He often had a play within a play. He had the people who were the directors teach you how to speak it "trippingly on the tongue." There are a lot of good instructions in what Shakespeare wrote about how to be a good speaker or actor. So if you would like to have Mr. Shakespeare teach you, just go down to the library. He's waiting for you."

The Author's Gift

Dottie always remembered the impact that libraries had on her and the books she read. Libraries are filled with many, many people of achievement.

Dottie knows that something of an author's spirit comes through in the books they write, because as she said, they wrote it for you! They really did. Those authors knew that you might need encouragement, guidance, insight, or hope. Those authors wrote of how they overcame challenges, struggles, and developed courage. Those authors could picture you reading that book being and uplifted with the words they wrote for you. That is why the author sweated, wrote, edited and worked hard to get that book into your hands. That author loved you.

From great minds through their books, we acquire in a few hours, what took the authors a lifetime to learn and discover. From reading two good books you gain two lifetimes of knowledge and learning. How valuable is that? I don't know about you, but most authors I choose to read have brilliant ideas and thoughts that expand me. They raise my learning curve, they expand my mind and expose me to thinking, knowledge, people and places that I didn't have the access to. Often those authors have a higher view that they want to show you. They get the big picture, and they will tell you how important you are to that big picture, because they know it's true. Many times while you read you will get an answer to a pressing question or dilemma you are facing. The author may be able to guide you a little further or quite a bit further along on your journey through life. I've read books that have inspired me so much that I changed how I did things or what I did. That has changed my life. Some of these "great minds" that Dottie mentions, she got to meet in person like Napoleon Hill, Dr. Norman Vincent Peale, and Bruce Barton. Great, great men.

Bruce Barton's Advice

Dottie told me one of the men who helped her tremendously was a very popular speaker named Bruce Barton who was widely known for a book he published about Jesus Christ in 1925 called "The Man Nobody Knows".

"Bruce Barton was a great mind and a great speaker," said Dottie. "He was the most famous speaker in America at that time, and I went to hear him speak. I went up afterwards and said to him, "I was so impressed with what you had to say, I feel like I learned so much from every word." He took my hand in

The Solution is at Hand, The Dottie Walters Story   111

his and said, "Oh, yes, I know who you are," and I said, "You do?" And Bruce said, "Yes, you're the one I came for."

"I thought, Wow! He understood right away what I was saying and that I got so much from it."

Those seven words deeply influenced her. She never forgot the lesson or the words.

Dottie often used the inspiring line Barton told her when she spoke. She passed along the message and gift from one of Americans finest speakers changing it slightly to "You're the one I wrote it for."

"They'll show me my book in shreds," Dottie told me. "It's just all worn out. Then I'll say, 'Well, you've been reading it." They say, "We just adore it and we hope you'll forgive that fact that it's in such bad shape.' I say, "It's not in bad shape because you are the one that I wrote it for. I know who you are."

It is wonderful that she has passed along Barton's great message and concern for people. Those messages live on through Dottie and touch even more people.

High on a Hill

One of the world's greatest thinkers, who wrote a book that has sold over ten million copies, with many more given away once it got into the public domain, was a friend of Dottie's – Napoleon Hill.

"Napoleon Hill was a tremendous man," Dottie remarked. "He saw me on a TV show that I was on – *To Tell the Truth*. He called up all of his friends to tell them to watch it."

I thought it was pretty amazing that Napoleon Hill told his friends to watch Dottie on TV. Can't you just picture the great author calling up and saying, "Watch Dottie Walters tonight on *To Tell the Truth*!" Napoleon Hill called Dottie after the show and said that just like the audience, Hill's wife wouldn't believe that Dottie was the one who wrote the book either. They were arguing about it. I told Dottie that he won that argument!

He asked Dottie to write the foreword to a book that he was writing. "I did that for him," she said. "We became really good friends. He was a kind, helpful man to people who were on their way up, just starting out in the business. He did several kind deeds to help me."

His book *Think and Grow Rich* was an amazing book. Dottie titled her second book *Speak and Grow Rich*.

Dottie said that she was thinking of his book and his title when she gave her best-selling book the name, *Speak and Grow Rich*, because she thought so much of him. Her book has become the premiere book for those interested promoting their professional speaking career.

Napoleon Hill loved and promoted Dottie's work. Here's what he wrote on her audio album *The Seven Secrets of Selling to Women*.

"How does it feel to be a girl who has just blown to the world a blast of inspirational stardust?"

The Mind of a Master

The great mind is always full of love and encouragement, like Dottie's grandfather was. He taught her to be strong, to keep going, to know that she was very valuable. Her grandfather had a grand mind. When someone is in pain, their emotions are strong. If you give them a big positive message right at that point, like her grandfather did, it does wonders for their self-esteem. Pick up the wisdom of some great minds. Build your own wisdom from their insights and encouragement as Dottie did. A good mind wants your mind to be better. They want to give you help. Take it! The solutions that you are looking for may be right in your own hands.

#3 Get Things Done Fast

Full Steam Ahead

When the audio book publisher wanted to publish Dottie's chapter, Dottie went ahead and had the cover designed the way she wanted even though they had their own idea. She got it done first and fast because she could see and visualize the book the way she wanted it to look. And of course, they loved it. Ask yourself how you can get things done fast?

The Good Speeding Ticket

Joe Vitale says that money likes speed, and I believe him. When you get an urge to act, act fast! Sometimes you must check things out first, but as you start to trust yourself, a power takes over to guide you and bring you success. If God came to the door and said, "Hi Jack, or Betty, or whoever you are, I need a ride to the airport," wouldn't you stop everything and take God to the airport, or church or where ever He wanted to go? God is asking you to look for your gifts. Use them, develop them, share them. God is calling you, as Dottie believes. He's giving you ideas. If you listen and act on them quickly you will find great success.

The hero column I write called *Heroes Among Us* started that way. I got the whole plan in a flash. I went to the paper and presented my idea to them. If I had waited I would have lost that matching moment and energy. If you wait to do things, you will lose that initial spark of excitement that was given to you to light a fire under your dream and get it moving. Dottie knows this secret.

Be fast
Set sail and raise the mast
Don't let your dreams settle in the past
Be fast!

#4 Pay Attention to the Good Voices

The Good Voice Choice

Dottie's grandfather gave her an excellent model of a good voice. Dottie put good voices into her mind to pull up whenever she needed to hear them. Dottie had a choice. She could have chosen to listen to her father's voice, which belittled her and discouraged her. It would have stopped her from succeeding. But she did not listen to that voice. She chose well. So can you. It really is your choice which voice you listen to. One of our greatest gifts is to choose. As my friend John Harricharan says, "We are here to learn how to make choices."

All of us, every one of us, has come in contact with a bad voice. All of us have also come in contact with the good voices. Let those good voices guide you to success. Find something inspirational from a good voice that you can use, as Dottie did with her grandfather words "Never give up, never give up." You can borrow those words if you wish. I'm sure Dottie wouldn't mind. Fill your life with good words and good messages. Then good things will start to come to you.

The voices you run into in life will be of all different heart levels. It is important to choose the positive ones to put into your life. The others are like junk food.

Dottie's grandfather also gave her a way to rationalize and handle big emotions. So when an equally big emotion came up, finding out there were no jobs at the newspaper, Dottie immediately "clicked" into her subconscious and the thought came in to never give up and look for the opportunity.

"It's up to you to open the door," says Dottie." See, no one can do it for you. Are you going to stand there forever and wait? So get going. Get going, because the world is waiting for you!"

Pay attention to each good voice
It's your decision, your Divine choice

Dottie's grandfather had a good voice. He inspired her to write "Drive the Dream," a poem in his honor. In this poem you will find many secrets to business success.

Dottie said, "This is a poem about my grandpa. I hope you will enjoy it. It's called *"Drive It!"*

Drive It
My Grandpa was a Scot... an Inventor,
"Creating's just the start... You must do more.
You hammer out the train. You lay down the track
From here to the end of the world and back.
"My ideas built the cars, but without the load
There's no profit for the crew. First the cargo's sold.
The Engineers are drivers, but they cannot go
'Till Management has figured it. Then the whistles blow!
"Life is like the railroad. You have to use your head
Watch for signals coming. Check that green or red.
Get your crew all ready, then stand by to leave.
Mastermind the system. Dream first, then Believe!
"Seize the wheels of commerce.
Push them 'round and 'round
Fire up your engine! Pull that Throttle down.
Double check your switches. Light your super-beam.
You're the Manager, My Darlin'
"YOU MUST DRIVE THE DREAM!"

#5 Don't Just Think, Take ACTION

Everyone Needs to be an Act-or

One of the many reasons Dottie admired Ben Franklin so much is not just because he came up with great ideas, but because he acted on them. He got results. He improved the world for others. That's a very good thing when we can make a better world. We can all think that way. Dottie did when she completed the covers for the audio book company in one week. She got ideas and then *did* something about them, like when she saw an advertisement about talking books and called the company right away. When you get an idea, do something with it. Some of your ideas might work, some might not, but you'll never know unless you take action.

Dottie looked at the word ACTION.

"A - To act is to do something positive and to never give up. Never give up, never give up. Remember that.

C - The "c" is to create something. People will say out of nothing, but you and I know that it wasn't "nothing." It was a great idea and you will recognize it as if it were your child, because you already know it's coming. Then you act on it.

T - And the third letter is "t" and that is thought. You can think forever. You know people who have been dreaming of doing something their entire life, and they never do it. It is the act. You have got to add the act and action to the thought, and now you've got something valuable.

I - And the next one is "i." Use your imagination. I think we are so lucky to have it. If you see pictures in your head – I do, and most of us do - don't think it's silly. Why do you suppose God gave you those pictures in your head? So you could visualize and create things. That's what you're supposed to do. That's how He made us.

O - The next letter is "o" for opportunity. You know what? It's always there when you act on it. If you take action and act on opportunity, my goodness, it appears like a magic wand!

N - That's when it's time to start. Not some day and some time, if I get around to it, DO IT NOW, because God's waiting. He gave you the job. Do it! You'll be surprised how much help He gives you. When you act, act well. It's better to take an action and do something positive, because then you'll get a result. If it needs to be improved, improve it. Every action you take maybe doesn't come out the way you thought it would to begin with. But if you work on it and improve it, it will grow, and grow, and grow. That's how all the great books were written, all the poetry, the music. It was all written by people who were taking action on something that God was giving them."

You can adjust if necessary and act again. You get more chances for success this way as long as you pay attention to whether that action puts you further or closer to your goal. Where do you take action? Look close, look close. That's what I did and I recommend it to you. People will see that you are taking action and you are working and trying. In my case we weren't going to lose that little track house. I wasn't going to let it get away from us after all my husband had gone through while away those four years in the South Pacific. He fought all those battles. We agreed. We were not going to lose the house!"

Where do you take action? Look close as Dottie did. She found opportunities in newspaper ads, magazines, everywhere. Listen to those thoughts. They are close by and close by will be the solution. Act on it.

It's a well know fact
To succeed you must act

The Solution is at Hand, The Dottie Walters Story   119

#6 Pull on the Rope Together

This is one of my favorite statements of Dottie's. At a time when it seemed hopeless, when her husband thought their house was lost because he didn't know what to do next, Dottie had a confident answer, "Let's pull on the rope together." If you get down or discouraged, find someone who can pull on that rope with you. Then the tug-of-war with life that seemed to stop you will start to make headway in your direction. Don't be afraid to ask for or give help. When you can help someone by pulling on the rope, or even pulling a few strings, choose to help lighten their load and distribute the energy of success evenly across that rope. When you help someone succeed, a problem has been solved. You have just found another solution.

"When you are with your husband, or your children, or whomever," says Dottie, "together you are going to get the job done. There is a great spirit that comes over you, because our Heavenly Father made us that way. He designed us with that in mind. We're going to help each other. It's a great feeling to do something together. Maybe you're building a house, or making a garden to grow some of the food you're going to eat. Whatever it is, work on it together."

Pull on the rope together
Pretty soon you'll find it's light as a feather

#7 Do Something Different Until You Find What Works

If Dottie had given up and had not given it that one last try to get Mr. Ahlman's approval, she may not have saved her home. She may not have believed in herself enough to start her business. How much less valuable the world would be without her books, speeches, magazine and her many God given gifts.

One Critical Last Try

Dottie said, "In the last try, it was critical that I sat down and tried to figure what to do next. You see, I wasn't *not* thinking, I *was* thinking! But she (Mrs. Ahlman) solved the problem for me by coming and sitting next to me. That one more try is what turned my whole column around. I filled it up every time. Pretty soon I was buying a second column because I had so many advertisers!"

Trying Changes No into YES!

Keep giving one more try until that try becomes success. How many of you could submit something 26 times and get a "No" and keep going until you succeeded? Dottie knew Edison never gave up, so she didn't either and magic happened. When you don't give up, it's as though there is an invisible force that sees your struggles and senses your determination to not quit. When it knows you are serious, it will come to your aid and give you what you want. Dottie knows this to be true, She certainly knows that if you set a true intent, give it your all and put your heart behind it, it has to be yours!

"Think of some of the great inventors," says Dottie. "For instance, Mr. Morse whose wife was deaf. He was trying to think of a way to make an invention that would help her. He loved her and he wanted to help her to hear. In doing so, he invented Morse code and radio. He invented that. Quite a marvelous man!"

If you do not stop you can succeed
For success likes determination, yes indeed

#8 Build a Strong Team Around You

Wall of Courage

Dottie started with a strong team - her children. She taught them to say, "Never give up!" She made it fun so that when a problem appeared, the children made it into a game to cheer her on to victory. Dottie creates the support around her for success. You too, must build support around you to succeed. Successful people know that there will always be some challenges and times of doubt when they will need to have built a wall of courage around them with their friends, families and employees. Have you done this for yourself yet?

Dottie loves the word *encourage*. It means with the heart. "The word *courage* comes from the French word "couer" for heart. Dottie had no trouble giving heart or encouragement to people. She knows that you don't wear out your heart by giving it away. "If you have *heart* you can accomplish anything!" said Dottie.

Often you build a wall of courage by encouraging others. That team will be there for you when you need the encouragement too. Or someone else will, because what goes around, comes around. You build a strong team by building others up. Your team will help you keep going to the solution that is waiting for you.

Build your team and make it strong
They'll cheer you on when things go wrong
So cheer them on!

#9 Look for the Lesson in Every Criticism

Understand criticism and you'll get the real story. When the woman came up to Dottie after her speech and said that she didn't like women speakers, Dottie didn't get defensive, she got curious. Dottie knew there was a story behind the woman's comments. She knew there was an opportunity there if she looked for it. Dottie acted with grace. Notice her amazing gift of compassion and action as she told how she took the woman's hands and understood the woman's concerns, but responded with a higher thought, "We women have to stick together." Dottie didn't agree with the woman's criticism of her, but she didn't argue with her either, or get defensive. She acknowledged her. Dottie gave her value.

The Gift of Appreciation

"To appreciate is to raise in value," says Dottie. "It's a lovely word to appreciate, isn't it? It also applies to people when you send a "Thank You" note to someone who has done something for you. Just tell somebody, 'Boy, I'm glad you're my mom,' or whatever it is you appreciate about someone. They don't forget that. It just touches their heart. So do it! Do it as much as you can."

The woman then told Dottie the incredible reason she stayed - because of the pink light all around Dottie. And as Dottie said, there was no pink light. The woman saw Dottie's love.

Dottie told me that when her children were growing up there was a special pink blanket at home. "We would sit around the dinning room table," she said. "If anybody had had a hard bump that day, they lost a ball game, they didn't get the grade they hoped they would, if they were feeling bad, or whatever it was,

124   The Solution is at Hand, The Dottie Walters Story

we had a pink blanket that we called the Love Blanket. We would say, 'You get the "Love Blanket" tonight."

That gave them encouragement to know that if they did have something that went wrong, that blanket was waiting. And now Dottie gives that to her audiences.

She said, "As I walk out on stage, I look at everybody and I hold my hands up, palms up. As I look at them, people to the left, people at the center, people across the room, I'm holding a "love blanket" in my hands. It's not a real one. You can't see it, but I see it. There are all kinds of things you can do by using the imagination and the mind. I get the feeling, and I know that you will too, that when you realize that God has given you a great thought that you can work with, you know it! It's just like He reached out and took your hand."

Think Pink

Your thoughts do project louder than the words you speak. "Love" and "I can help you," were the underlining messages that Dottie gave to her audiences. That is what they feel and remember. People can see the thoughts you have. Dottie thinks that is very exciting. She knows it to be true. She also knows that is also your responsibility to choose your thoughts as you speak for we can feel thoughts. People can feel what you are thinking. If someone criticizes you, respond with understanding. Know that it isn't about you. There might be an opportunity for understanding and better communication. Fill yourself up with love. Surround yourself with a pink blanket when you go into a situation where you might be tempted to get defensive. Don't react to criticism. Act and react, and react again...with love.

Surround yourself with love in all you do
And love will be reflected back to you
Your thoughts speak louder then the words you say
Let them both match and go the same way

The Solution is at Hand, The Dottie Walters Story   125

#10 Two Wrongs are Still Wrong

Poetic Remarks

Dottie told the story of a man who first stole a poem she wrote, then passed it off as his own. In addition to that, he added an insult by saying that Dottie couldn't have possibly written that poem herself. He assumed that Dottie had also stolen the poem, therefore justifying his nasty behavior. What is interesting is how Dottie reacted. First, notice again her amazing curiosity. She asked him, "I see you are using my poem." Initially she didn't assume the worst, but gave him a way out. He did not take it. What if, instead of the remark he gave, he had said, "I'm sorry I didn't ask you first. May I have your permission to quote your lovely poem?" Dottie said she would have helped him. Boy did he blow a big opportunity! This man lost a golden chance to be helped by a woman who went on to achieve enormous success. Dottie said he never made it in the speaking business. Of course not! Audiences see through that false front. You can't fool them. People who do things that are wrong, usually try to make others wrong too. They can even get indignant. It's a false front. Hold your ground when you're in the right.

"When you do something wrong and you realize it, instantly correct it and make loving amends," says Dottie. "You'll feel better right away, and so will the person who's feeling bad because they thought you were their friend. Now they are feeling hurt about it. You'll both feel better and that's a two-way, good thing."

It's a win-win.

Be strong – admit you're wrong
Go on to success, where you belong

#11 Look at How Observant Children Are

Children are deeply affected for good or bad by what you say to them and how you treat them. Throughout the CD "The Dottie Walters Story: The Solution is at Hand" Dottie mentions something several times: children and their enormous curiosity, their thirst for fun and knowledge, and their profound sensitivity.

When Dottie was young, her father hit her to teach her math. Well, that didn't work! We don't learn by force, but by kindness and caring. That's how she chooses to treat her audiences. She could have passed on what she received, but she was too good and wise for that. Dottie remembers clearly her grandfather's kindness and the lessons he taught. Remember how Dottie taught her children to say "Never give up"? Those kids were sharp. They got a lesson and they knew exactly when to use it. Sometimes adults think children don't have feelings or don't understand, but children are remarkably wise. Dottie knew that.

Look at what a little entrepreneur she was at 3 or 4 years old selling sand dollars for pennies. That wisdom would hold up at any boardroom across the nation.

Dottie's First Poem

"When I was 8 years old," Dottie said, "my mother and father drove to Chicago from California because there was a great big World's Fair up there. We went out to the children's section. They had what looked like a mountain that you could see from across the fairgrounds. I think they called it the Magic

Mountain. You went inside and went round and round walking up to the top. When you got to the top, then you got to come down on this great big slide. Oh, was that exciting! You went *whoom* down to the bottom, where your mother and everybody was waiting for you. Then they presented each child with a little toy copy of these buses. So I got to bring one home. I loved that so much.

On the way home, driving all the way back across the country, I had a poem come into my mind. I found a piece of paper and a pencil in the back seat, and I asked my mother to write down what I had thought of. She said, 'You know, Dorothy, I think we'll send this to *Wee Wisdom Magazine.*' They always had great stories. I usually didn't have enough money to buy it, until I found enough bottles that people put out by their trash. They were a penny apiece if you took them back to the store. When I got enough (about 15 cents) I got to buy a copy of the magazine. I never threw one away. I read them all. I had them all memorized. I loved them so much. So at 8 years old, I had my first poem published. Oh, was that ever a thrill!"

Here is that poem:

The World's Fair

When I went to the Fair, you see,
The Enchanted Isle appealed to me.
Ponies, cars, trains and boats so small
Were there at the children's beck and call
And puppet shows and movies, too.
Oh, something fine for all to do.
The magic mountain was a scare,
As it towered high up in the air.
I climbed to the top and looked around,

128   The Solution is at Hand, The Dottie Walters Story

Then down a tree trunk came with a bound.
A coaster wagon was there to see,
With baby wagons as cute as could be.
And "teensy" buses, the Fair's own kind,
To take to the ones we left behind.
The time was so short.
Now, who was to blame?

"I talked about the tiny buses of the fair's own kind, to bring to the one you left behind," said Dottie. "I don't remember who the "left behind" person was. A friend of mine, I guess, that I brought it back for. I gave it to them because they didn't get to go."

That's just like Dottie – always thinking of someone else. Be aware as Dottie is of how wise children are. Treat them with respect. You never know when that wisdom and encouragement might be just what YOU need!

It's true that children have developing minds
But you will find their hearts wise and big and kind

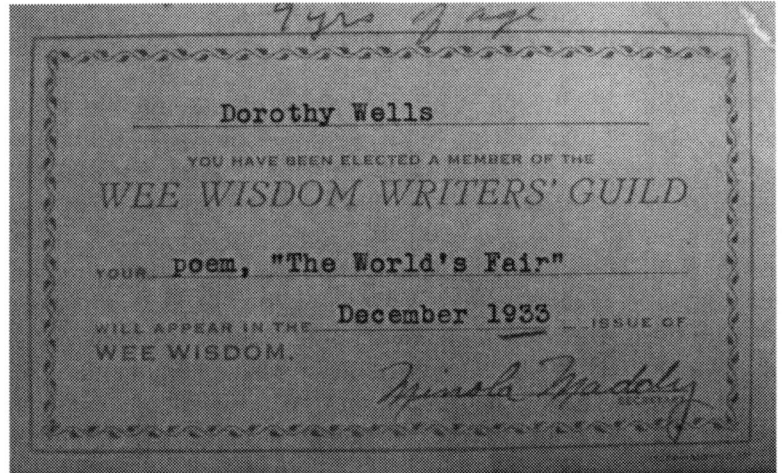

#12 The Best Story You Can Tell is Your Own

Your Story is Your Glory

Dottie is great at telling stories of all kinds, but the story that we most love to hear is her story of pushing her babies to the soda fountain in the drug store to save the family home. The soda fountain story is Dottie's story and no one else's. No one can tell it the way she can. Every one has unique experiences. It is those experiences that happen specifically to you, the ones that impact you, that can have an impact on others as well, especially if you tell your story in an intriguing and lively manner. What if Dottie had told her soda fountain story the following way?

"We needed money so I went to the pharmacist in town and finally got him to buy some ads." We'd go, Ho hum. It's the same facts, but it has no heart. Instead, Dottie brought us right there with her, in her desperate state, pushing babies, holes in her shoes, wheels coming off, feeling dejected when the pharmacist first turned her away, but finding the courage to not give up. Boy, did she describe a scene!

Dottie said, "If you tell your own story in a loving way, in a caring way, so that you'd like to give someone else a hand, they know it. They feel it. You are broadcasting it to them from your heart to theirs. I promise you, they will feel it."

Pretend the story that you want to tell is a radio show. Pretend people can only hear you. They can't see you. Do they get a clear picture from your words? Do they understand how you feel? Do they wonder what you did next? Make it real for them and bring them right into it. No one can deliver that story like you can. Use this in your speeches, your businesses, your ads, or any human communication.

The story tells
and the story sells

While working on this CD, Dottie's story, her message so inspired me that I wrote a poem for her about the soda fountain story where she discovered success called *The Fountain of Opportunity*.

The Fountain of Opportunity

for my good friend Dottie Walters

She sat at the soda fountain, Coke in her hand
She'd waited for the word from the pharmacist man
He held the key to her success that she surely did know
Pushing her babies to his drug store on that road so long ago
When the stroller broke down and off came the wheels
She took her cardboard-lined shoes and struck with her heel
"We NEVER give up!" she taught the children to cheer
And she pushed on along with her goal held clear
He shook his head when she pled her case
And she saw rejection all over his face
What could she do without his consent
Of her shopper's column, what that "Yes" would've meant?
But as she sat to ponder, an angel sat down too
And looked her in the eyes and said, "Girl, what's wrong with you?"
She tried to keep her spirits up, but told her of her plight
Her need for this man's blessings on the column she held tight
She'd done all she could when that woman took that seat

At the curved wooden stool by that mother young and sweet

The woman looked at the column, read each and every word

And with a voice commanding, yelled so everyone had heard

"Rueben get out here!" and the pharmacist obeyed

Before he knew what happened, two months of advertising had been paid!

So her fountain saved that home, now in her home it rests

When the grand woman of opportunity passed her biggest test

#13 You Create by Visualizing

Dottie knows a deep secret - that the things we accomplish, do and create in our lives, we first create in our minds. It is by seeing it first in our mind's eye, that we take the actions necessary to with see it with our physical eye.

"Being able to visualize is a great gift," said Dottie. "A painter can't paint that picture until he looks at that canvas and he sees what he wants to happen. Sometimes they draw a very light sketch with a pencil. Then they go ahead and start doing the colors and so forth, but they saw it complete from the beginning."

"That's a great gift and we all have it. Don't knock yourself down and say, "Oh yes, but I don't." Stop doing that! YES, YOU DO!

"I remember when I was a little girl, one day my mother took me to see *Peter Pan* in a theater. It was a matinee, and oh, I just loved that! I wished that they would do it again and again and again! But they, of course, they did that one performance so I didn't get to see it again, and again. My mother told me that there was a book on Peter Pan at the library, and she got it for me. I was able to read it, and my goodness, I saw that play over and over again IN MY HEAD, because I had seen it and was reading about it!"

The library is a source that both Dottie and I have used tremendously. The libraries are free. They are there for all of us. Even it people don't think that they have other assets, the library with all that knowledge is there for everyone of us.

"I have always made very strong pictures in my mind," said Dottie. "My mother used to go next door and do a little grocery shopping, leaving me at the library, which I loved. They had a little children's table with a stereopticon which you could look through and see the picture. It made it look 3-dimensional. She came back to get me one day and I was wailing and crying. She said, 'What's the matter?' I said 'They are hurting that poor girl.' It was Joan of Arc! Of all things to give children in the library! They were putting her on the stake with the fire and all. I heard the crackling and I was there!"

This is the Art of Creation

"I think that is one of the greatest gifts that God gives us. That is the ability to visualize. Every piece of music, every poem, every movie, somebody's visualizing that. Then they make it come true. When people can see the picture in their mind that you have in yours, you are a great communicator."

When I was struggling to find a new place to live, Dottie used visualization with a very powerful effect. It was a great gift to me. "I will hold a picture in my mind of you in a beautiful new place," she said to me. When someone of her caliber creates a mental picture with their highly developed and aware mind, boy does magic happen! Her confidence was catching. The next day I found my new home.

When I thanked Dottie for doing that visualization of my new place she said, "There is a whole group of creative fairies that march around up there and look for things like that."

Dottie said, "I think that God visualizes each of us as he gives us the set of gifts he has for us."

Picture This

"When you see a picture, " said Dottie, "it gets the message through to your subconscious mind. The subconscious uses images to create your life. You are the artist. People who are in the speaking world, sometimes forget that anybody who is an actor knows how to project the picture in their mind. When you see the lights go out and then a flashlight comes across the screen, you think maybe it's a burglar or something. Everybody is going, "Look out! Look out!" They see the burglar. Maybe there's nothing but the light going on by the electrician. Maybe there isn't anybody there, but they know how to create the illusion. Once you can get those pictures in your mind where you can see them clearly, then if it's writing a poem, writing a song, painting a picture, whatever it is, get those pictures. Realize that that is the way you create things. Was there ever anything that wasn't created this way? For instance, Edison was trying to find the filament for the light and he thought of something Einstein had said "The solutions are always at hand." Edison noticed a little bamboo fan that he was using in his laboratory, and he thought Bamboo! He tried it and it worked! It was already in his hand! That close!"

"Pictures are the clay of the mind. And you have to do something with it, create it for it to work. But it's wonderful, It's fun. Ask any artist and they will tell you."

Stone Decisions

Dottie loves this story and describes it in such a charming way.

"A long time ago there was a boy who lived in Rome. He wanted to take sculpting lessons. He begged his mother for them He ran errands, and did all kinds of jobs to help her. She finally got the money together to buy the lessons for him. He noticed that out in back of the sculpting shop was a great big piece of marble but

The Solution is at Hand, The Dottie Walters Story   135

it was cracked and all bent over. He went out and stared and stared at it. One day he said to his teacher, 'What are you going to do with that piece of marble?' The teacher said, 'Well it's no good. We are going to break it up and throw it away.' The boy said, 'Please don't do that. I see something in it.' The teacher said, 'What do you see?' The boy said, 'I see the great spirit of courage.' The teacher said, 'All right. Go ahead."

"Little by little by little, the boy took away what was already there in the marble. And what was there was the statue, "David" with the slingshot. But the idea was that the boy was able to create something that would give other people courage just by looking at it. A little boy (David) who would stand there to battle the giant. When he took away the stone, everybody saw that he had talent. His name was Michelangelo."

"I can see him standing up there and seeing what's in the stone. That's true of everything that we want to accomplish in life. If you want to start a business, if you want to write a book, whatever it is you want to do, you've got to visualize it in your mind, and pretty soon you'll actually put it together, because you can see it! If you can see it, you can do it."

Get a picture nice and clear

Very soon it will appear

And the main lesson Dottie says she has learned in life is:

#14 Help is Always Close By

"It's at hand," she says. "Every problem has a solution. EVERY PROBLEM."

Whatever you are facing now, help is close. Whatever seemingly impossible endeavor you are undertaking, hope is always there.

Hot and Cold

There is a fairy tale about a king asking throughout the land for a recipe that would contain both hot and cold. Chef after chef throughout the kingdom tried and failed, until one chef came and brought ice cream with chocolate hot sauce on it. An ice cream sundae! And the king, obviously with a sweet tooth, loved it. The chef's neck was saved.

There's another story I've always loved. It's about Mother Theresa. She said, "Hold out your hand." She touched each finger and gave five words, "God is always with you." Dottie knows that too. She has trust, deep faith, loyalty, compassion, the ability to see beyond the pettiness right into the heart. She looked for guidance and expected it. Like a heroine in a movie, her next steps seemed to appear. Yours can too, when you learn and apply these lessons from Dottie.

Dottie said we both benefited from doing this project together because we both learned from each other. "That's the way with life, isn't it?" she said. I certainly believe so.

In true Dottie Walters fashion, she thanked me telling me what a joy it was to work on this project with me. I'd certainly have to add humility to her many fine character traits.

In your journey through life and the many adventures you will have, remember to ask for and look for the solution - the one God created especially for you and for the problems you face. You will find that every problem comes with a perfect solution.

Wishing you lots of success and joy in finding your solutions. And a reminder from Dottie, "Remember where solutions are located. They are always at hand."

We hope that you have enjoyed The Solution is at Hand, The Dottie Walters Story and you rediscover the word *hope* in your life. May you be excited about opportunities that are everywhere for you. And may you enjoy every moment in the great game of life

When prospects seem bleak and options seem few

Remember this advice being offered to you

Don't give up when discouragement looms

Or shower with predictions of doubt and gloom

There is always a way, God has it planned

For as Einstein once said, "The Solution is at Hand!"

May you find a solution to your every problem!

Dottie Walters

Terri Marie

Epilogue

Dottie Walters
Dec 31, 1924 to Feb. 14, 2007
New Year's Eve to Valentine's Day

The Delays

We knew we didn't have much time and had been working day and night to get this book finished as quickly as possible. Every one was helping, from the book designers to John Harricharan of New World Publishing, so that Dottie could hold this book in her hands. Delay after delay occurred. For some reason it seemed no matter what we did, no matter how hard we tried, something else would come up.

Finally the book was ready. Then a suggestion came (and a very good one) from Yanik Silver –– to make a few changes on the title. John Harricharan also had a great idea to have the foreword written by someone who knew and loved Dottie. Through a very quick series of serendipitous events, I contacted my friend Ken Druck, who was friends with Jack Canfield. Our mutual friend John Assaraf immediately forwarded the request to Jack Canfield, and Jack contacted me the next day. He agreed and to write the foreword, even though he was busy preparing for a visit on Oprah to talk about *The Secret*. Dottie loved Jack Canfield. It was perfect.

The Journey

I had planned to leave for California immediately to get the book to Dottie. Everything was set on my table to pack up the next morning. That night, I had a dream that Dottie had passed away. They were wheeling her through a door. Pushing the dream out of my mind, I woke and got ready.

It was early Valentine's Day and I was anxious to see Dottie. The phone rang. It was Michael, her grandson. When I asked him how he was, he said, "Not so good. Dottie just passed away." I was stunned. The very day I was to see her. I was devastated to get the call, but I knew Dottie wanted was ready to leave. She knew the book was completed. She had delivered her message. Her work was done.

As I sat there shocked, I heard a strange sound. It was a plane. Small planes rarely fly over the area where I live. The tiny white plane flew past my window but something was different and strange about it. I looked harder. The little plane had golden wings! I knew Dottie was sending me a message. She was OK. She was flying high now.

The preview copy of the book was in California, so I made the drive to pick it up. Once in my hands, I took our book to the nature center instead of to Dottie as I had intended. A woman walked over and asked me "What are you reading? Is it good?" "I hope so." I said. "I just finished writing it." With Dottie's words and message in my hand, I found a beautiful, gentle brook and sat beneath the redwoods to read our new creation.

I asked for another sign from Dottie. Driving back from reading her book, out of nowhere, a yellow balloon floated directly in front of my car and hovered there. I didn't see it come. I didn't see it leave. Just the few seconds when in floated in front of my car. That happened once more. The appearance of the yellow balloon. Dottie's sign.

The Book's Life

After Dottie passed away, I emailed our mutual friend Jack Nichols. Jack called me right away. I told him that I was disappointed Dottie didn't get to see the finished book. Jack said, "You didn't write the book just for Dottie. Dottie knew that. You wrote the book for the people who didn't get to meet Dottie. She knew you'd get it to them and deliver her work." You, dear reader, are special. Dottie had this book written for you.

The Bagpipes Came

Dottie would've been pleased with her memorial service. There were family, friends, speaker bureau owners, NSA Board members, and noted professional speakers, all of whom Dottie had helped or inspired. Even members of audiences that Dottie had recently spoken to showed up, touched by the great gift she gave of herself. Everyone spoke of Dottie's profound influence on their lives. They were each given a copy of this book. Many held the book as they got up to speak about Dottie - like a connection to her very soul. When I asked Dottie about her ability to help others, she told me, "It was in them all along - I just shined the light."

There is an exercise which many workshops include that asks you to write what people will say at your funeral. If we could all live lives that touched and inspired as many people in such profound ways as Ms. Walters, I don't think it'd be too long before we'd turn this world around. Dottie had chosen what she wanted me to say at her service. One day when I came to the ranch, I read her a part of the book and she said, " I want you to read that at my funeral."

They played Dottie's beloved bagpipes as we left the church. On the altar was a photo of Dottie standing in front of the Crystal Cathedral waving and smiling. Dottie had loved talking to the Speakers Bureau that evening. Oh how she charmed them! But after awhile she tired. She had taken a bad fall a few months earlier and was still recovering. A year earlier we'd gone to a Book Publicist meeting in Hollywood and drove back later that night. Dottie got up at 4:00 AM the next morning to catch a plane to the East Coast for an entire weekend seminar! I didn't know how she had that kind of energy. Dottie used every precious minute of her life.

Ready to Go Home

Dottie missed her husband Bob terribly. While we were doing the interviews, I had wanted to ask her a few more questions. Dottie was having a bit of trouble with questions that day, until I mentioned a question about Bob. She immediately slumped down. Her entire energy dropped. She said, " I just miss him so much." I stopped the interview.

Dottie had a deep belief in the presence of the "other side." Bob and Dottie often "talked" at night in her dreams. Once she was concerned about a project she had to complete. Dottie related to me that Bob had said to her, "Don't worry honey. You did just fine."

The night of February 13th, 2007, Michael MacFarlane told me he had made Dottie dinner and later that evening he was making sure she was comfortable and covered up. He said Dottie had a different air about her that night. Dottie asked Michael over and over, "Michael, when is your Grandfather (Bob) coming to pick me up? When is Bob coming to get me?" Dottie died that next morning at 4:47 AM. Bob, I'm sure was delighted to be "picking up" his beloved wife. Michael said Bob never missed a Valentine's Day with Dottie even if he had to fly to Australia to see her.

During the last few months, Dottie slept a lot and didn't eat much. Often, I'd bring her patty melts on my way to the ranch and we'd have lunch together, but there were many times when she couldn't eat anything. Yet she never complained. I knew I was witnessing the presence of a truly great being. Every time anyone would come to visit, she would smile delighted. "I'm so glad you came." She was tired, and most likely in pain, yet her focus was always on the other person. It was amazing and humbling to see her do this.

"I know God hears our prayer," she told me. When I told her I was praying for her, she always thanked me. Once she asked me for 105 prayers. I asked her why 105? "Oh, I think that's a good number," she replied.

Her Legacy

Because she was one of the best speakers in the world, something rubbed off on those around Dottie. She was a tremendous help in teaching me about speaking, and providing expert guidance in setting my fees and getting my speaking career ready. Dottie showed me what speaking was – sharing your message.

Dottie and I often went to listen to other speakers together. However, when we went to these meetings, it seemed as if she was struggling to walk. I didn't want to offend her, but once I gently asked her if she wanted to take my arm. She did. We walked arm in arm around the lake at The Sportsman's Lodge in Hollywood. She pointed out the beautiful swans, telling me they mate for life, like her and Bob. Later as she got weaker, back at the ranch, she would show me pictures of Bob – her Marine. We'd walk back arm in arm to her family room, the place where she felt most comfortable resting.

Dottie loved the people who worked with her. She constantly praised Deborah Acero her secretary and had enormous confidence and trust in her. Sally Isenberg was new on staff, but Dottie was happy to have her aboard. Jim McJunkin, who lived on the ranch, helped Dottie with projects and was a joy to her. If someone treated Dottie right, she never forgot it.

In this book, we couldn't possible list everything Dottie accomplished in her life. She even inspired people at 30,000 feet when she was taped for American Airlines broadcasts. Dottie was a born leader, but she also inspired leadership in others. That's rare. She knew that leaders have to be the ones who look out for others – that's the key. Dottie gave undivided, charming attention, yet had sincerity and humility at the highest level I've ever seen.

I looked through my notes from my talks and meetings with Dottie. Right there up at the top of the first page from that first meeting were the words, "The Solution is at Hand." It was capitalized. This was from 2004.

Dottie was the best cheerleader I ever knew. "You're on your way kid" she'd say after I followed through on something she had suggested I do. (I'm hardly a kid!) Because Dottie placed so much trust in me, I knew that I could never let her down. When

144   The Solution is at Hand, The Dottie Walters Story

someone of her level puts their faith in you, they live in you. Your soul has expanded with the essence of a great person. Dottie never got to hold the actual finished book in her hands but I know she is smiling and holding it in her wings.

I shall miss the walks with Dottie. The frail arms of her grand spirit. I shall miss the phone calls every weekend. Two weeks before she died, the phone calls stopped. She could no longer get to the phone. But even to the very end, she had brilliant messages. Here is one of them:

"It's always been my philosophy… let's make the audience happy."
Dottie Walters 1/28/07

I shall miss those times. I shall miss her beautiful voice. But she will always be with us. Dottie has entered into the realm she so loved and relied upon. She has become a Friend of the Mind. May she forever be your friend too. That would make Dottie very happy.

Terri Marie

" In trailing clouds of glory shall I return to my Creator, only to find that I had never really left. I shall walk among the lilies of the field and leave my trail in stardust in the sky."
–John Harricharan

Dottie Walters

Dottie Walters is one of the worlds premier sales and motivational speakers. She began a tiny advertising business on foot, pushing her babies in a broken down baby stroller, in a rural community with no sidewalks. She built that business into 4 offices, 285 employees, and 4,000 continuous contract advertising accounts. Dottie sold this large business to concentrate on her own speaking, giving seminars, writing, and publishing her own newsmagazine, "Sharing Ideas."

She is the author of 5 books including, Never Underestimate the Selling Power of a Woman (Wilshire Book Co). Speak & Grow Rich with Lilly Walters, (Prentice Hall-Simon Schuster). The Greatest Speakers I've Ever Known (WRS Publishing), 101 Simple Things to Grow Your Business and Yourself: Easy Ideas to Improve Sales, Productivity and Service!, with Lilly Walters, (Crisp Publishers, July, 1995), and Chicken Soup for the Soul, 2nd. Helpings"(featured author in the books and videos)

Dottie has created countless audio recordings and held many "Speak & Grow Rich: The Seminar" Master weekends at her ranch in Glendora, CA. She is a consultant and has written numerous articles for publications around the world. Dottie was interviewed by: CNN, ABC, "Good Morning Australia," "Good Morning South Africa, and many other TV shows. She was featured on American Airlines Business Channel on all Domestic and International Flights, and on SKY radio broadcast to major cities and to United and Delta Airlines passengers. Interviewed on hundreds of radio shows, and by newspapers and magazines around the world. Dottie Walters hosted a regular radio program for National Business Radio Network on the subject of great business ideas that was heard in 75 major cities in the United States.

Her role as publisher/editor of "Sharing Ideas" Newsmagazine made the magazine the top international publication in the paid speaking field. A world-class speaker and favorite with audiences in the U.S., England, Malaysia, Australia, Japan, Canada, and South Africa. Today Dottie is President of Walters Speakers Services. She founded the Professional Association for Speakers Bureaus, International Group of Agencies & Bureaus (IGAB); Recipient of IGAB's John Palmer Award for outstanding contributions to the bureau industry.

Dottie was a Founding Member of the National Speakers Association, Founder of the Los Angeles Chapter NSA, Life Board Member, and past National Board Member.

Terri Marie

Author, Speaker, Producer, Creativity Expert

Terri Marie is a Producer of 26 documentaries, several ski films and hosted an exercise program called, "The Great Body Escape." She was a winner of the 2005 Pinnacle Award for Best Self-Help book (Be the Hero of Your Own Game) from North American Bookdealers and received a 2005 Irwin Award in the Humanitarian category from The Book Publicists of Southern California. Her second book, "One Minute Inspirations" is about to be published by New World Publishing.

She produced music and has written over a thousand of her own songs, dozens of articles published in magazines around the world and appeared in *Success* Magazine. Her song, "Reagan's Ride" was performed eight days after Former President Reagan's death at the Nixon Presidential Library.

Called the "Poetress of San Clemente," she is known for coming up with a poem or song instantly to fit the occasion. Her poem, "Eye Don't Care," about hurricane Katrina's devastation was published in 2005. Terri Marie writes a monthly column, "Heroes Among Us," for the Orange County Register, Sun Post News. The column's goal is to raise awareness of what all of us can do to become heroes.

Terri Marie loves to help people with their beliefs, especially their belief in themselves and their ability to succeed. She says "the game of life was designed for all of us to win. We are all meant to be heroes." In her seminars and playshops, she helps ignite the creative spark within us all.

**Here are some of the poems Dottie and I
had a great time writing.**

And a Bear in an Avocado Tree
© 2005
Terri Marie

Down the mountain wall he lopes
'Cross gladed glen and slanted slopes
His prickled fur twitches, it tickles the brush
Low plants sink flat, then rebound from his touch

His eye set for the fruit of an avocado tree
In the yard of the woman they know as Dottie
Could he be bound for the Scottish clan, this bold bear
With lumbering limbs and shiny black hair?

Oh great giant one
Round pirate of the arbor
Down from your high abode
Roaming from your mountain harbor

On his fine restaurant seat in the air
Sits the mighty big bear
Served a green nightly feast
Of precious avocado meat

He dines up there with the birds and the bees
Munching his green prizes delightfully
As merry as an old great bear can be
But can the branch hold his vast body? Barely.

We do worry Mr. Beast so fine
If you have crossed the weight limit line
No branch we would foresee of the sweet fruit tree
Fallen, while carrying its bear company
While you determinedly fill your grand belly

So neatly full with pear shaped green jelly
Chewing the candy of the avocado tree
We have a tip to give, you see

Leave the climbing to cats and creatures like that
Who can perch the bough light and happily
And go to your cave, avocado depraved
Who's heard of a bear in a little fruit tree?

So dear creature
Before my avocado tree is bare too
Please come down
You're blocking my view

Here Is Genius
The Geni-in-us
Dottie Walters

Some say genius is a person
But the Ancients state, "Not so.
Genius is a river's mighty flow.
"There is more of it behind its dam
Than ever flows before.
The channels always gushing, pouring more."

To open Genius's floodgates
Fill your mind with dreams.
Bar the door to "no" and "how it seems."

Allow your thoughts to wander;
Search for signs of what-can-be!
Then plan and work, and use your industry.

For the genius River's rising;
Heartbeat, close it pounds – at hand!
        Like the Geni of the lamp who shouts:
                    "Command!"

Quick Order Form
Walters Speakers Services

Telephone orders: Call 626-335-8069
Email orders: sharingorders@aol.com

Postal Orders:
Walters Speaker Services
P.O. Box 398
Glendora, CA 91740

Please send me _____ copies of "The Solution is at Hand: The Dottie Walters Story"

Name:_____

Address:_____

City:_____State_____ZIP_____

Telephone:_____

Email:_____

I would like a gift copy sent to:

Name:_____

Address:_____

City:_____State_____ZIP_____

Paperback is $14.95
Shipping is $5.00 within Continental USA
Each additional book to same address is $2.50
Sales Tax: Please add 8.25% for CA residents

For other books such as the best selling "Speak and Grow Rich" and "Never Underestimate the Selling Power of a Woman" and products or to order Sharing Ideas Magazine go to:
www.Speakandgrowrich.com

Quick Order Form
White Wing Entertainment

Telephone orders: Call 714-926-8948
Email orders: terrimarie@herobookonline.com

Postal Orders:
White Wing Entertainment
P.O. Box 3325
Sedona, AZ 86340

Please send me _____ copies of "The Solution is at Hand: The Dottie Walters Story"

Name:_____
Address:_____
City:_____State_____ZIP_____
Telephone:_____
Email:_____

I would like a gift copy sent to:

Name:_____
Address:_____
City:_____State_____ZIP_____

Paperback is $14.95
Shipping is $5.00 in the Continental US
Each additional book to same address is $2.50
Sales Tax: Please add 8.550% for Arizona residents

Award–winning BE THE HERO OF YOUR OWN GAME is $16.95 paperback.
For other books and products to help you on your journey through life go to: www.spiritualarena.com

Author Terri Marie is available for consulting. Email: terrimarie@herobookonline.com
Get a FREE inspirational message for a full year! A $150 value.
Sign up for your **"Year of Cheer"** at www.herobookonline.com

Remember...
The solution is
always at hand!